Diabetic LIVING Holiday COOKING VOLUME 10

DIABETIC LIVING® HOLIDAY COOKING
IS PART OF A BOOK SERIES
PUBLISHED BY BETTER HOMES AND
GARDENS SPECIAL INTEREST MEDIA,
DES MOINES, IOWA

Cranberry
Crumble Bars,
p. 145

From the Editors

Haul out the holly and turn on the oven. 'Tis is the season for holiday gatherings with family and friends. This recipe collection brings a new spin on traditions with food that inspires you to take control of your eating and feel better, too.

You'll find breakfast delights, holiday breads and appetizers, spectacular main dishes, unforgettable sides, and guilt-free desserts. Among them are simple recipes, too, for those crazy-busy days. And the whole family will love them!

Each recipe has been tested for accuracy, ease of preparation, and great taste. All feature complete nutrition information to make it easy for you to track calories, carbs, fat, and sodium to meet your meal-plan goals.

Helpful tips sprinkled throughout suggest ways to avoid holiday weight gain, save time, and reduce stress. It's designed to help you celebrate your most delicious, most relaxed, and healthful holidays yet.

ON THE COVER
Expresso Custards, *p. 142*

Photographer
BRIE PASSANO
Food Stylist
JENNIFER PETERSON
Art Director
SHELLEY CALDWELL

18

59

118

Diabetic LIVING Holiday COOKING VOLUME 10

CONSUMER MARKETING

Vice President, Consumer Marketing	STEVE CROWE
Director of Direct Marketing–Books	DANIEL FAGAN
Marketing Operations Manager	MAX DAILY
Assistant Marketing Manager	KYLIE DAZZO
Senior Production Manager	AL RODRUCK
Contributing Project Manager	SHELLI MCCONNELL, PURPLE PEAR PUBLISHING, INC.
Contributing Art Director	SHELLEY CALDWELL
Contributing Food Stylist	JENNIFER PETERSON
Photographer	BRIE PASSANO
Test Kitchen Director	LYNN BLANCHARD

DIABETIC LIVING® MAGAZINE

Editorial Director	JESSIE PRICE
Executive Editor	LAUREN LASTOWKA
Creative Director	JAMES VAN FLETEREN
Associate Editor	MICAELA YOUNG, M.S.
Managing Editor	WENDY S. RUOPP, M.S.

MEREDITH NATIONAL MEDIA GROUP

President, Consumer Products TOM WITSCHI

President and Chief Executive Officer TOM HARTY

Vice Chairman MELL MEREDITH FRAZIER

Diabetic Living® Holiday Cooking is part of a series published by Meredith Corp., 1716 Locust St., Des Moines, IA 50309-3023.

If you have comments or questions about the editorial material in *Diabetic Living® Holiday Cooking*, write to the editor of *Diabetic Living*, Meredith Corp., 1716 Locust St., Des Moines, IA 50309-3023. Send an email to *DiabeticLiving.Specials.com*

Diabetic Living® magazine is available by subscription or on the newsstand. To order a subscription to the magazine, go to *dlvcustserv@cdsfullfillment.com*

Rosemary-
Almond
Cookies,
p. 150

CONTENTS

1

EYE-OPENING
BREAKFASTS

Make this first meal merry with color and flavor. Add bright veggies to scrambled eggs for a tasty upgrade. Or skip the stirring and bake a fancy oatmeal to warm a chilly morning. These dishes set the table with deliciousness while keeping carbs low. Ingredients like pumpkin spice, rainbow chard, and winter pear add a holiday touch.

18

23

27

Egg, Kale, and Mushroom Casserole

casserole stand at room temperature 30 minutes and preheat oven to 350°F. Uncover and bake 50 to 60 minutes or until internal temperature reaches 160°F. If necessary, cover with foil the last 10 minutes of baking to prevent overbrowning.

PER SERVING *(1⅓ cups each)* **CAL** 256, **FAT** 11 g *(4 g sat. fat)*, **CHOL** 140 mg, **SODIUM** 505 mg, **CARB** 23 g *(4 g fiber, 6 g sugars)*, **PRO** 17 g

"Egg in a Hole" with Avocado Salsa

14g
CARB

SERVES 4
TOTAL 35 min.

- 2 medium bell peppers, any color
- 1 medium avocado, halved, seeded, and finely chopped
- ½ cup finely chopped red onion
- 1 fresh jalapeño chile pepper, seeded and finely chopped (tip, p. 154)
- ½ cup chopped fresh cilantro
- 2 medium tomatoes, seeded and finely chopped
- 2 Tbsp. lime juice
- ¾ tsp. salt
- 2 tsp. olive oil
- 8 eggs
- ¼ tsp. black pepper

1. Slice tops and bottoms off bell peppers; finely chop. Remove and discard seeds. Slice each pepper into four ½-inch-thick rings.
2. For salsa, in a bowl combine chopped bell pepper, the next six ingredients (through juice), and ½ tsp. of the salt.
3. In a large nonstick skillet heat 1 tsp. of the oil over medium. Add four of the bell pepper rings; crack one egg into the middle of each ring. Season with ⅛ tsp. each salt and black pepper. Cook 2 to 3 minutes or until the whites are mostly set but the yolks are still runny. Gently turn and cook until desired doneness (1 minute more for runny yolks; 1½ to 2 minutes more for firmer yolks). Transfer to plates and repeat with the remaining pepper rings, eggs, salt, and black pepper.
4. Serve with avocado salsa and, if desired, garnish with additional cilantro.

PER SERVING *(2 filled pepper rings each)* **CAL** 285, **FAT** 19 g *(5 g sat. fat)*, **CHOL** 372 mg, **SODIUM** 589 mg, **CARB** 14 g *(6 g fiber, 6 g sugars)*, **PRO** 15 g

Egg, Kale, and Mushroom Casserole

23g
CARB

SERVES 6
HANDS ON 30 min.
TOTAL 1 hr. 25 min.

Nonstick cooking spray
- 1 Tbsp. olive oil
- 2 8-oz. pkg. fresh cremini mushrooms, sliced
- 1 cup thinly sliced red bell pepper
- ¾ cup chopped onion
- 4 cloves garlic, thinly sliced
- 1 6-oz. pkg. baby kale, coarsely chopped
- ¾ cup fat-free milk
- 4 eggs
- 2 egg whites
- 1 Tbsp. Dijon-style mustard
- ½ tsp. black pepper
- ¼ tsp. salt
- 6 oz. crusty whole grain bread, cut into 1-inch cubes
- ¾ cup shredded Gruyère or Swiss cheese (3 oz.)
- ¼ cup crumbled feta cheese (1 oz.) (optional)

1. Preheat oven to 350°F. Coat a. 2-qt. baking dish with cooking spray. In an extra-large nonstick skillet heat oil over medium-high. Add mushrooms, bell pepper, onion, and garlic; cook about 15 minutes or until mushrooms are dark brown and vegetables are tender, stirring occasionally. Stir in kale; cook 2 to 3 minutes or until kale just wilts.
2. Meanwhile, in a medium bowl whisk together the next six ingredients (through salt).
3. Place bread cubes in the prepared baking dish. Top with vegetable mixture and Gruyère cheese. Pour egg mixture over top; press down lightly with the back of a large spoon so all the bread is moistened.
4. Bake 45 to 50 minutes or until top of casserole is browned and a knife inserted in center comes out clean (160°F). Let stand 5 minutes before cutting. If desired, top with feta cheese.

TO MAKE AHEAD Prepare as directed through Step 3; cover and refrigerate up to 12 hours. Before baking, let

"Egg in a Hole" with Avocado Salsa

Cauliflower and Sausage Hash with Eggs

To make your own, place 2 cups cauliflower florets at a time in a food processor and pulse until chopped into rice-size pieces. One 2-lb. head of cauliflower makes about 4 cups of cauliflower rice.

PER SERVING *(about 1 cup hash + 2 eggs each)* **CAL** 317, **FAT** 19 g *(5 g sat. fat)*, **CHOL** 415 mg, **SODIUM** 654 mg, **CARB** 8 g *(3 g fiber, 3 g sugars)*, **PRO** 26 g

---

Sweet Potato Hash Brown Nests

16g
CARB

SERVES 8
HANDS ON 25 min.
TOTAL 55 min.

- 1 tsp. canola oil
- 5 cups peeled and coarsely shredded sweet potatoes
- 1 cup finely chopped onion
- 1 tsp. garlic powder
- 1 tsp. dry mustard
- ½ tsp. salt
- 2 tsp. cornstarch
  Nonstick cooking spray
- 4 thin slices prosciutto, halved crosswise
- 8 eggs
- ¼ cup shredded cheddar cheese (1 oz.)
- 8 cherry tomatoes, quartered
- ¼ cup thinly sliced green onions

1. Preheat oven to 400°F. In a large nonstick skillet heat oil over medium-high. Add next five ingredients (through salt). Cook about 8 minutes or until potatoes are beginning to brown, stirring occasionally. Remove from heat. Stir in cornstarch.
2. Lightly coat eight 2½-inch muffin cups with cooking spray. Press about ¼ cup potato mixture onto bottom and up sides of each prepared muffin cup. Bake 10 minutes.
3. Line potato cups with prosciutto. Break an egg into each potato cup. Sprinkle with cheese. Bake about 12 minutes more or until egg whites are completely set and yolks are thickened. Remove from muffin cups. Top with tomatoes and green onions.

PER SERVING *(1 nest each)* **CAL** 172, **FAT** 7 g *(3 g sat. fat)*, **CHOL** 192 mg, **SODIUM** 398 mg, **CARB** 16 g *(2 g fiber, 4 g sugars)*, **PRO** 11 g

---

Cauliflower and Sausage Hash with Eggs

8g
CARB

SERVES 4
HANDS ON 15 min.
TOTAL 25 min.

- 4 tsp. olive oil
- ⅓ cup finely chopped onion
- 2 cloves garlic, minced
- 8 oz. ground turkey sausage
- 4 cups cauliflower rice
- 3 Tbsp. water
- ¼ tsp. salt
- ⅛ tsp. black pepper
- 8 eggs

1. In a large nonstick skillet heat 2 tsp. of the olive oil over medium. Add onion and garlic; cook until translucent, stirring often. Add sausage; cook 4 to 5 minutes or until cooked through, stirring occasionally. Transfer to a plate.

2. Increase heat to medium-high. Add cauliflower rice to the pan in an even layer. Cook, without stirring, 2 to 3 minutes or until it starts to turn golden brown. Stir in the water, salt, and pepper. Cover and cook 3 to 4 minutes or until tender and golden. Stir in the sausage mixture and heat through.
3. In a medium nonstick skillet heat 1 tsp. of the oil over medium. Break four of the eggs into the skillet. Cook about 3 minutes or until whites are set but yolks are still runny (or up to 5 minutes for firmer yolks). Transfer to a plate and repeat with the remaining 1 tsp. oil and remaining four eggs.
4. Divide the cauliflower and sausage hash among four plates and top each with two fried eggs.

TIP Look for cauliflower rice in the freezer section of your supermarket.

Sweet
Potato
Hash Brown
Nests

Rainbow
Chard
Spanish
Tortilla

Rainbow Chard Spanish Tortilla

14g CARB

SERVES 6
HANDS ON 1 hr.
TOTAL 1 hr. 40 min.

- 1 8-oz. bunch rainbow chard
- 5 large eggs
- 4 large egg whites
- ½ tsp. salt
- ½ tsp. black pepper
- 12 oz. Yukon Gold potatoes, cut into ¼-inch-thick slices
- 2 Tbsp. olive oil
- ½ cup chopped onion
- 6 cloves garlic, minced
- 2 oz. fresh chorizo sausage
- 3 Tbsp. grated Manchego cheese

1. Preheat oven to 350°F. Remove chard leaves from stems. Chop the stems. Stack the leaves and coarsely chop. Set both aside separately.
2. In a medium bowl whisk together eggs, egg whites, salt, and pepper.
3. Place potatoes in a 4-qt. pot and add 1 cup water. Bring to boiling; reduce heat. Cover and simmer 5 to 10 minutes or until potatoes are tender. Drain.
4. In a large ovenproof nonstick skillet heat 1 Tbsp. of the oil over medium-high. Add half of the potatoes to the pan; cook to 2 to 3 minutes per side or until browned. Transfer to a large bowl. Repeat with the remaining potatoes.
5. Heat the remaining 1 Tbsp. oil in the pan. Add chard stems, onion, and garlic. Cook 4 to 6 minutes or until tender, stirring occasionally. Stir in the chard greens; cook 1 to 2 minutes or until wilted. Transfer chard to bowl with potatoes. Add chorizo to pan; cook 3 to 5 minutes or until cooked through, stirring to break up chorizo. Transfer chorizo to bowl with potato mixture; toss gently to combine. Spoon the potato-chorizo mixture into the skillet. Pour the egg mixture over top; sprinkle with cheese.
6. Bake about 25 minutes or until the top is lightly browned and the center is set. Let stand 15 minutes. Invert a large plate over pan. Using oven mitts, grasp pan and plate together and invert so that the tortilla falls onto the plate. Cut tortilla into 6 wedges.

PER SERVING *(1 wedge each)* **CAL** 201, **FAT** 11 g *(3 g sat. fat)*, **CHOL** 163 mg, **SODIUM** 433 mg, **CARB** 14 g *(2 g fiber, 1 g sugars)*, **PRO** 12 g

Tomato-Parmesan Mini Quiches

Tomato-Parmesan Mini Quiches

5g CARB

SERVES 6
HANDS ON 25 min.
TOTAL 50 min.

- Nonstick cooking spray
- 12 4-inch round thin slices lower-sodium cooked ham
- 1¼ cups seeded and chopped roma tomatoes
- ½ cup thinly sliced green onions
- 1 Tbsp. chopped fresh basil or 1 tsp. dried basil, crushed
- ¼ tsp. black pepper
- ⅔ cup finely shredded Parmesan cheese
- 6 eggs, lightly beaten

1. Preheat oven to 350°F. Coat twelve 2½-inch muffin cups with cooking spray.
2. Line prepared muffin cups with ham. Divide tomatoes, green onions, basil, and pepper among cups. Top with cheese. Pour eggs into cups.
3. Bake 20 to 25 minutes or until puffed and a knife inserted in centers comes out clean. Cool in cups 5 minutes. Remove from cups. If desired, top with additional green onions and/or fresh basil. Serve warm.

PER SERVING *(2 mini quiches each)* **CAL** 159, **FAT** 8 g *(4 g sat. fat)*, **CHOL** 207 mg, **SODIUM** 450 mg, **CARB** 5 g *(1 g fiber, 3 g sugars)*, **PRO** 15 g

Confetti Hash Browns and Eggs

33g
CARB

SERVES 4
TOTAL 30 min.

- 2 tsp. olive oil
- 1 cup chopped onion
- 2 cups chopped red, orange, green, and/or yellow bell peppers
- 1 cup finely chopped broccoli
- 2½ cups frozen diced hash brown potatoes, thawed
- 1 tsp. chopped fresh thyme
- 1 tsp. Worcestershire sauce
- ½ tsp. salt
- ¼ tsp. black pepper
  Dash hot pepper sauce
- 4 eggs

1. In a large nonstick skillet heat oil over medium. Add onion; cook 2 minutes. Add bell peppers and broccoli; cook about 4 minutes or until vegetables are crisp-tender, stirring occasionally. Stir in the next six ingredients (through hot pepper sauce). Cook, covered, over medium about 12 minutes or just until potatoes are tender and golden, stirring occasionally.

2. Using a large spoon, make four indentations in potato mixture. Break an egg into each indentation. Cook, covered, 4 to 5 minutes more or until whites are completely set.

PER SERVING (¾ cup hash browns + 1 egg each)
CAL 240, **FAT** 8 g (2 g sat. fat), **CHOL** 186 mg, **SODIUM** 417 mg, **CARB** 33 g (4 g fiber, 4 g sugars), **PRO** 11 g

Savory Egg
and Sweet
Potato
Scramble

Savory Egg and Sweet Potato Scramble

20g CARB

SERVES 4
TOTAL 35 min.

8 eggs
⅓ cup milk
½ tsp. ground cumin
¼ tsp. salt
¼ tsp. black pepper
1 Tbsp. butter
2 medium sweet potatoes, peeled, quartered lengthwise, and sliced
2 Tbsp. sliced green onion
2 cups fresh baby spinach
Fresh Italian parsley
Hot pepper sauce (optional)

1. In a medium bowl whisk together eggs, milk, cumin, salt, and pepper.
2. In a large skillet melt butter over medium. Add sweet potatoes and green onion. Cook about 8 minutes or just until potatoes are tender and light brown, stirring occasionally. Add spinach; cook and stir about 1 minute more or until slightly wilted.
3. Pour egg mixture over potato mixture in skillet. Cook over medium, without stirring, until egg mixture begins to set on bottom and around edges. Using a spatula or large spoon, lift and fold partially cooked egg mixture so uncooked portion flows underneath. Continue cooking 2 to 3 minutes or until egg mixture is cooked through but is still glossy and moist. Remove from heat.
4. Sprinkle with parsley. If desired, serve with hot pepper sauce.

PER SERVING (1¼ cups each) **CAL** 258, **FAT** 13 g (5 g sat. fat), **CHOL** 381 mg, **SODIUM** 390 mg, **CARB** 20 g (3 g fiber, 5 g sugars), **PRO** 15 g

Corncakes and Eggs

31g CARB

SERVES 6
HANDS ON 25 min.
TOTAL 45 min.

⅔ cup all-purpose flour
⅔ cup yellow cornmeal
2 tsp. baking powder
⅛ tsp. salt
1¼ cups buttermilk

Corncakes and Eggs

½ cup refrigerated or frozen egg product, thawed, or 2 eggs, lightly beaten
2 Tbsp. canola oil
1 cup shredded reduced-fat cheddar cheese (4 oz.)
4 green onions
2½ cups chopped tomatoes
1 Tbsp. lemon juice
⅛ to ¼ tsp. black pepper
Nonstick cooking spray
6 eggs
¼ tsp. salt
⅛ tsp. black pepper

1. For batter, in a medium bowl stir together flour, cornmeal, baking powder, and the ⅛ tsp. salt. Make a well in center of flour mixture. In a small bowl combine buttermilk, the ½ cup egg, and oil. Add egg mixture to flour mixture; stir just until moistened. Fold in ½ cup of the cheese. Transfer to a heavy resealable plastic bag.
2. Thinly slice green onions, separating white and green parts. For salsa, in a medium bowl combine white parts of onions, tomatoes, lemon juice, and the ⅛ to ¼ tsp. pepper.
3. Lightly coat a nonstick griddle with cooking spray; heat griddle over medium. Snip a ½-inch hole in

a bottom corner of bag with batter. Working in batches, pipe 6-inch rings of batter onto hot griddle. Quickly break a whole egg into each ring and sprinkle with some of the ¼ tsp. salt and ⅛ tsp. pepper. Cook 3 to 4 minutes or until surfaces of corncakes are bubbly. Turn corncakes and sprinkle with some of the remaining ½ cup cheese. Cook 1 to 2 minutes more or until corncakes are golden and yolks are desired doneness. Remove from griddle; keep warm while cooking the remaining corncakes. Serve with salsa and green parts of onions.

TO MAKE AHEAD Corncake batter, salsa, and green parts of onions can be stored in the refrigerator up to 3 days. To make individual corncakes, divide batter among six small, heavy resealable plastic bags before storing in refrigerator. To serve, pipe one bag of batter onto hot griddle and break one whole egg into the ring; cook as directed. Top with 6 Tbsp. of the salsa and about 1 Tbsp. of the green parts of onions.

PER SERVING (1 corncake + 6 Tbsp. salsa each) **CAL** 325, **FAT** 15 g (5 g sat. fat), **CHOL** 202 mg, **SODIUM** 629 mg, **CARB** 31 g (2 g fiber, 5 g sugars), **PRO** 18 g

Sheet Pan Frittata with Rainbow Chard

6g CARB

SERVES 6
HANDS ON 10 min.
TOTAL 55 min.

- 3 Tbsp. olive oil
- 1 16-oz. bunch rainbow or Swiss chard (tip, *below*)
- 1 cup cherry tomatoes, halved
- ¼ cup thinly sliced shallot
- ¼ tsp. salt
- 12 eggs
- 1 cup refrigerated unsweetened plain almond milk
- ¼ tsp. black pepper
- ¼ cup chopped fresh herbs, such as basil, oregano, and/or Italian parsley

1. Preheat oven to 375°F. Brush bottom and sides of a 15×10-inch baking pan with 2 Tbsp. of the oil; place pan in oven 5 minutes. Meanwhile, remove chard leaves from stems. Chop the leaves (you should have about 8 cups). Trim and thinly slice the stems (you should have about 2½ cups). Add stems to the baking pan. Roast 5 minutes. Add chopped chard, tomatoes, shallot, salt, and the remaining 1 Tbsp. oil to pan. Toss to coat. Roast about 10 minutes or until chard is wilted and tomatoes soften, stirring once.
2. Meanwhile, in a large bowl whisk together the eggs, milk, and pepper. Pour egg mixture over vegetables in pan, spreading evenly.
3. Bake about 20 minutes more or until egg mixture is set. Let stand 10 minutes. Cut into squares, then triangles to serve. If desired, top with fresh herbs and additional roasted tomatoes.

PER SERVING (⅙ frittata each) **CAL** 234, **FAT** 17 g (4 g sat. fat), **CHOL** 372 mg, **SODIUM** 432 mg, **CARB** 6 g (2 g fiber, 2 g sugars), **PRO** 15 g

QUICK TIP

For a milder flavor, substitute 8 cups fresh spinach for chard. Toss spinach with tomatoes, shallot, 1 Tbsp. olive oil, and salt. Roast as directed in Step 1.

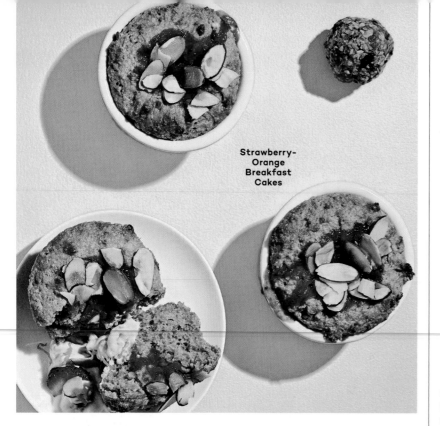

Strawberry-
Orange
Breakfast
Cakes

Orange-Scented Whole Grain Pancakes

36g CARB | SERVES 6
| TOTAL 30 min.

- 1½ cups white whole wheat flour
- 3 Tbsp. flaxseed meal
- 1½ tsp. baking powder
- ½ tsp. baking soda
- ¼ tsp. ground ginger
- ⅛ tsp. salt
- 3 oranges
- 1¼ cups buttermilk
- 2 eggs
- 1 tsp. vanilla
- 2 Tbsp. packed brown sugar
- 2 Tbsp. canola oil

1. In a large bowl whisk together the first six ingredients (through salt).
2. Remove 1 Tbsp. zest from one of the oranges. Sqeeze ¼ cup juice from the orange. Cut the remaining two oranges into segments. Cut the segments into thirds.
3. In a medium bowl whisk together orange juice, orange zest, and the remaining ingredients. Add the orange mixture to the flour mixture; stir until just combined. Do not overmix. Let batter stand 5 minutes.
4. Lightly coat an extra-large nonstick pan or griddle with cooking spray. Heat over medium-high. Working in batches, spoon ⅓ cup batter per pancake into the hot pan. Cook 3 to 4 minutes or until pancakes begin to bubble. Turn pancakes and cook 2 to 3 minutes more or until lightly browned.
5. Keep pancakes warm in a 200°F oven until ready to eat. Serve with the reserved orange segments.

PER SERVING (2 pancakes + ½ cup orange segments each) **CAL** 248, **FAT** 9 g (1 g sat. fat), **CHOL** 64 mg, **SODIUM** 399 mg, **CARB** 36 g (5 g fiber, 11 g sugars), **PRO** 9 g

Strawberry-Orange Breakfast Cakes

35g CARB | SERVES 6
| HANDS ON 25 min.
| TOTAL 55 min.

- ⅔ cup white or regular whole wheat flour
- ½ cup oat bran
- ¼ cup almond meal or white or regular whole wheat flour
- 1½ tsp. baking powder
- ¼ tsp. baking soda
- ¼ tsp. ground cinnamon
- ⅛ tsp. salt
- ¾ cup vanilla fat-free yogurt
- ¼ cup packed brown sugar
- ¼ cup refrigerated or frozen egg product, thawed, or 1 egg, lightly beaten
- 2 Tbsp. vegetable oil
- ½ tsp. almond extract (optional)
- 1 orange
- ¼ cup low-sugar strawberry preserves
  Nonstick cooking spray
- 3 Tbsp. sliced almonds
- ⅓ cup chopped fresh strawberries
- ⅓ cup vanilla fat-free yogurt

1. Preheat oven to 375°F. For batter, in a medium bowl stir together the first seven ingredients (through salt). In a small bowl combine the next five ingredients (through almond extract). Stir egg mixture into flour mixture just until combined.

2. For filling, remove zest (if desired) and squeeze 1 Tbsp. juice from orange. Set zest aside. In a small bowl combine orange juice and preserves.
3. Coat six 6-oz. custard cups or ramekins with cooking spray; set cups in a shallow baking pan. Spoon ⅓ cup batter into each prepared cup. Bake about 10 minutes or until edges are firm but centers are still slightly doughy. Remove from oven. Spoon filling onto cakes; sprinkle with almonds. Bake about 9 minutes more or until a toothpick inserted in centers comes out clean. Cool on a wire rack 10 minutes.
4. For topping, in a small bowl combine strawberries and ⅓ cup yogurt; spoon onto warm cakes. If desired, sprinkle with orange zest.

TO MAKE AHEAD Prepare as directed through Step 2. Store batter, orange zest, and filling in separate airtight containers in refrigerator up to 3 days. To prepare one cake, preheat oven to 375°F. Spoon ⅓ cup chilled batter into one prepared 6-oz. custard cup or ramekin. Bake as directed, using about 1 Tbsp. of the filling and 1½ tsp. of the almonds. Serve with 1 Tbsp. of the topping.

PER SERVING (1 cake + 1 Tbsp. topping each) **CAL** 229, **FAT** 9 g (1 g sat. fat), **CHOL** 1 mg, **SODIUM** 265 mg, **CARB** 35 g (3 g fiber, 16 g sugars), **PRO** 7 g

Orange-Scented Whole Grain Pancakes

Puffed
Oven-Baked
Pancakes
with Fruit

Puffed Oven-Baked Pancakes with Fruit

14g
CARB

SERVES 6
HANDS ON 10 min.
TOTAL 25 min.

Nonstick cooking spray
3 eggs, lightly beaten
6 Tbsp. all-purpose flour
6 Tbsp. fat-free milk
1 Tbsp. sugar
Dash salt
⅔ cup fresh fruit, such as blueberries or sliced pineapple, strawberries, peeled peach or kiwifruit, nectarine, and/or pear
1 Tbsp. orange marmalade
Fat-free Greek yogurt and/or chopped fresh mint (optional)

1. Preheat oven to 400°F. Lightly coat twelve 2½-inch muffin cups or six 10-oz. custard cups or gratin dishes with cooking spray.
2. In a small bowl combine eggs, flour, milk, sugar, and salt until smooth. Immediately pour batter into prepared muffin cups. Bake 15 to 20 minutes or until pancakes are puffed and golden. (Pancakes will puff up and sink quickly.)
3. Meanwhile, wash and dry bowl. Add fruit and marmalade; toss to coat.
4. Top puffed pancakes with fruit mixture and, if desired, yogurt and/or mint. Serve warm.

PER SERVING (2 pancakes each) **CAL** 96, **FAT** 3 g (1 g sat. fat), **CHOL** 93 mg, **SODIUM** 69 mg, **CARB** 14 g (1 g fiber, 7 g sugars), **PRO** 5 g

Pumpkin-Spiced Breakfast Bread Pudding

Pumpkin-Spiced Breakfast Bread Pudding

36g
CARB

SERVES 8
HANDS ON 20 min.
TOTAL 3 hr.

Nonstick cooking spray
12 oz. baguette-style French bread, cut into 1-inch cubes and dried
1½ cups fat-free milk
1 cup refrigerated or frozen egg product, thawed, or 4 eggs, beaten
1 cup canned pumpkin
⅓ cup packed brown sugar
1 tsp. pumpkin pie spice
4 oz. reduced-fat cream cheese (neufchatel), cut into small cubes
½ cup coarsely chopped pecans, toasted
1 tsp. powdered sugar

1. Coat a 2-qt. rectangular baking dish with cooking spray. Arrange bread cubes in the prepared dish.

2. In a large bowl combine the next five ingredients (through pumpkin pie spice). Slowly pour egg mixture over bread cubes; press lightly with the back of a large spoon to moisten. Dot with cream cheese cubes. Cover with plastic wrap and chill 2 to 24 hours.
3. Let bread pudding stand at room temperature 30 minutes. Preheat oven to 350°F. Uncover dish. Bake 30 to 35 minutes or until center is puffed, golden, and registers 160°F near the center. Remove from oven. Let stand on a wire rack 10 minutes. Just before serving, sprinkle with pecans and powdered sugar.

TIP To dry bread cubes, preheat oven to 300°F. Place bread cubes in an ungreased 15×10-inch baking pan. Bake 12 to 15 minutes or until dry and crisp, stirring once or twice.

PER SERVING (¾ cup each) **CAL** 262, **FAT** 8 g (2 g sat. fat), **CHOL** 11 mg, **SODIUM** 354 mg, **CARB** 36 g (2 g fiber, 14 g sugars), **PRO** 9 g

Raspberry Breakfast Parfaits

32g CARB

SERVES 4
HANDS ON 20 min.
TOTAL 45 min.

Nonstick cooking spray
4 **cups regular rolled oats**
⅓ **cup shredded coconut**
¼ **cup sliced almonds**
¼ **cup dry-roasted unsalted sunflower kernels**
¼ **cup honey**
3 **Tbsp. canola oil**
2 **Tbsp. packed brown sugar**
½ **tsp. ground cinnamon**
1 **cup plain fat-free yogurt**
2 **Tbsp. orange marmalade**
1 **cup fresh raspberries**
Fresh raspberries (optional)

1. Preheat oven to 350°F. Coat a 15×10-inch baking pan with cooking spray. To make granola, in a medium bowl combine oats, coconut, almonds, and sunflower kernels. In a small bowl combine honey, oil, brown sugar, and cinnamon. Drizzle honey mixture over oat mixture. Stir until oats are coated.
2. Spread oat-honey mixture evenly in the prepared pan. Bake about 25 minutes or until lightly browned, stirring twice.
3. Line a large baking sheet with foil or parchment paper. Spread baked granola on prepared baking sheet; set aside to cool. Store in an airtight container at room temperature up to 1 week.
4. To make parfaits, in a small bowl combine yogurt and marmalade.
5. Place about 2 Tbsp. of the raspberries in each of four 10-oz. glasses. Top each with about 2 Tbsp. of the yogurt mixture. If desired, stir gently to mix. Add about 2 Tbsp. of the granola to each glass. Repeat layers, but do not stir. If desired, top with additional raspberries.

PER SERVING *(1 parfait each)* **CAL** 196, **FAT** 6 g *(1 g sat. fat)*, **CHOL** 1 mg, **SODIUM** 59 mg, **CARB** 32 g *(4 g fiber, 18 g sugars)*, **PRO** 7 g

QUICK TIP

If you don't have time to make the granola, substitute your favorite healthful purchased granola.

Baked Oatmeal with Pears

38g
CARB

SERVES 6
HANDS ON 20 min.
TOTAL 1 hr.

Nonstick cooking spray
2 **cups old-fashioned oats**
½ **cup walnuts, chopped**
2 **tsp. ground cinnamon**
1 **tsp. baking powder**
¾ **tsp. salt**
¼ **tsp. ground nutmeg**
⅛ **tsp. ground cloves**
2 **cups refrigerated unsweetened plain almond milk or 2% milk**
1 **cup plain low-fat Greek yogurt**
¼ **cup pure maple syrup**
2 **Tbsp. olive oil**
1 **tsp. vanilla**
2 **cups finely chopped pears**

1. Preheat oven to 375°F. Coat a 2-qt. square baking dish with cooking spray.
2. In a large bowl stir together the next seven ingredients (through cloves). In a medium bowl whisk together the next five ingredients (through vanilla). Pour the wet ingredients into the dry ingredients. Gently mix in pears.

Transfer the mixture to the prepared baking dish.
3. Bake 45 to 55 minutes or until golden brown. If desired, top each serving with 1 Tbsp. additional yogurt.

TIP Both ripe and unripe pears work in this recipe; however, unripe pears will hold their shape better during cooking.

PER SERVING (⅙ casserole each) **CAL** 311, **FAT** 15 g (2 g sat. fat), **CHOL** 4 mg, **SODIUM** 449 mg, **CARB** 38 g (5 g fiber, 15 g sugars), **PRO** 9 g

Ginger-
Acai Bowls
with Almond-
Pepita
Clusters

Ginger-Acai Bowls with Almond-Pepita Clusters

32g CARB | **SERVES** 4
HANDS ON 20 min.
TOTAL 45 min.

- 1 egg white
- 1 to 2 Tbsp. honey
- ¼ tsp. kosher salt
- ½ cup sliced almonds
- ½ cup pumpkin seeds (pepitas)
- ½ cup unsweetened large coconut flakes
- 2 Tbsp. flaxseed meal
- 2 bananas, peeled, sliced, and frozen
- 1 cup frozen mixed berries
- ½ cup plain low-fat Greek yogurt or unsweetened kefir
- ½ cup low-fat milk, water, or fruit juice
- 2 2-oz. packets frozen unsweetened acai puree
- 1½ tsp. grated fresh ginger
  Topper(s): sliced banana, berries, and/or chopped mango, peach, kiwifruit, or pineapple

1. Preheat oven to 325°F. Line a 15×10-inch baking pan with parchment paper. In a large bowl lightly whisk together egg white, honey, and salt. Stir in almonds, pumpkin seeds, coconut, and flaxseed meal. Spread in the prepared baking pan. Bake about 25 minutes or until golden, stirring once; cool.
2. In a blender combine next six ingredients (through ginger). Cover and blend until smooth, adding 1 to 2 Tbsp. additional milk if needed to reach desired consistency. Serve in chilled bowls with desired topper(s) and 1 cup of the nut clusters.

TIP If using kefir, do not add the ½ cup milk, water, or fruit juice.

TIP Look for acai puree in the freezer section or online. To naturally sweeten the puree, blend it with frozen sweet fruits such as bananas, blueberries, strawberries, cherries, or dates.

TIP You won't use all of the almond-pepita clusters. Store extras, covered, at room temperature up to 1 week. Use as a snack or salad topper.

PER SERVING (¾ cup smoothie + ¼ cup nut clusters + toppers each) **CAL** 251, **FAT** 11 g (3 g sat. fat), **CHOL** 4 mg, **SODIUM** 85 mg, **CARB** 32 g (7 g fiber, 18 g sugars), **PRO** 10 g

Berry-Mint Kefir Smoothies

Berry-Mint Kefir Smoothies

27g CARB | **SERVES** 2
TOTAL 5 min.

- 1 cup plain low-fat kefir
- 1 cup frozen mixed berries
- ¼ cup fresh orange juice
- 1 to 2 Tbsp. fresh mint
- 1 Tbsp. honey

1. Combine all ingredients in a blender. Cover and blend until smooth, scraping sides as needed.

TO MAKE AHEAD Cover and refrigerate mixture up to 24 hours. To freeze, transfer mixture to a freezer container and freeze up to 3 months.

PER SERVING (1 cup each) **CAL** 137, **FAT** 1 g (1 g sat. fat), **CHOL** 5 mg, **SODIUM** 64 mg, **CARB** 27 g (4 g fiber, 15 g sugars), **PRO** 6 g

2 TASTY PARTY BITES

Wow your family and friends with a spread of finger foods and small bites. Pumpkin, cranberries, and champagne are just a few ingredients that add yuletide flavor pops while keeping calories, fat, and carbs light. When the doorbell rings, you'll be relaxed and ready to let your guests nosh, sip, and mingle.

34

40

44

Prosciutto-
Wrapped
Honey-Lemon
Shrimp

Cajun-Spiced
Wings with
Honey Glaze

Prosciutto-Wrapped Honey-Lemon Shrimp

5g
CARB

SERVES 8
HANDS ON 40 min.
TOTAL 45 min.

- 24 fresh or frozen jumbo shrimp in shells (about 1 lb.)
- 1 lemon
- 2 Tbsp. honey
- 2 tsp. chopped fresh parsley
- 6 very thin slices prosciutto (4 to 5 oz.)

1. Thaw shrimp, if frozen. Preheat broiler. Peel and devein shrimp, leaving tails intact. Rinse shrimp; pat dry with paper towels. Place shrimp in a large bowl. Remove ½ tsp. zest and squeeze 2 Tbsp. juice from lemon. In a small bowl combine lemon zest and juice, the honey, and parsley. Pour over shrimp; toss gently to coat.
2. Cut prosciutto slices in half crosswise and then in half lengthwise (24 pieces total). Wrap a piece of prosciutto around each shrimp; secure with a wooden toothpick.
3. Place shrimp on the lightly greased unheated rack of a broiler pan. Broil 4 to 5 inches from heat 4 to 6 minutes or until shrimp are opaque and prosciutto is crisp, turning once.
4. If desired, sprinkle shrimp with additional lemon zest and chopped fresh parsley. Serve with additional honey for dipping.

PER SERVING *(3 shrimp each)* **CAL** 84, **FAT** 4 g *(0 g sat. fat)*, **CHOL** 32 mg, **SODIUM** 283 mg, **CARB** 5 g *(0 g fiber, 4 g sugars)*, **PRO** 8 g

Cajun-Spiced Wings with Honey Glaze

13g
CARB

SERVES 8
HANDS ON 15 min.
TOTAL 35 min.

- 16 chicken wing drummettes (2 lb. total)
- 2 Tbsp. salt-free Cajun seasoning
- ½ cup ketchup
- ¼ cup lemon juice
- ¼ cup honey
- 1 tsp. ground mustard

1. Preheat oven to 450°F. Line a 15×10-inch baking pan with foil. In a large bowl toss together chicken and 5 tsp. of the Cajun seasoning. Arrange chicken pieces in prepared pan. Bake 15 minutes; turn wings. Bake 15 to 20 minutes more or until chicken is no longer pink.
2. In a large bowl stir together the remaining 1 tsp. Cajun seasoning, the ketchup, lemon juice, honey, and mustard. Transfer half of the mixture to a serving bowl. Add chicken to the remaining sauce in the bowl. Toss to combine.
3. Transfer chicken wings to a foil pan and place on a grill rack over direct medium heat. Cover and grill 10 to 15 minutes or until heated through. Serve with remaining sauce.

TIP If you can't find salt-free Cajun seasoning, stir together 1 Tbsp. paprika; 1 tsp. each onion powder and garlic powder; ½ tsp. each dried oregano, crushed, and dried thyme, crushed; and ¼ tsp. each black pepper and cayenne pepper.

TO MAKE AHEAD Prepare as directed through Step 2. Transfer chicken and reserved sauce to separate airtight containers. Cover and chill up to 3 days. Continue as directed.

PER SERVING *(2 drummettes each)* **CAL** 182, **FAT** 9 g *(2 g sat. fat)*, **CHOL** 78 mg, **SODIUM** 184 mg, **CARB** 13 g *(0 g fiber, 12 g sugars)*, **PRO** 13 g

Cranberry-
Orange-
Glazed Turkey
Meatballs

QUICK TIP

To keep meatballs and
sauce warm for serving,
transfer to a 5- to 6-qt.
slow cooker and set
to warm setting.

Cranberry-Orange-Glazed Turkey Meatballs

20g CARB

SERVES 10
HANDS ON 40 min.
TOTAL 50 min.

Nonstick cooking spray
- 1 Tbsp. olive oil
- 2 medium carrots, finely chopped
- 1 stalk celery, finely chopped
- ½ cup finely chopped onion
- 1 cup reduced-sodium chicken broth
- ½ cup bulgur
- ⅓ cup + 2 Tbsp. water
- 2 eggs
- 1½ tsp. ground coriander
- 1 tsp. salt
- ¼ tsp. black pepper
- 1¼ lb. ground turkey
- 1 cup canned whole-berry cranberry sauce
- ⅓ cup orange juice
- 2 tsp. cornstarch
- ⅛ tsp. cayenne pepper

1. Preheat oven to 400°F. Coat a 15×10-inch baking pan with cooking spray.
2. In a large skillet heat oil over medium. Add carrots, celery, and onion. Cook 4 to 5 minutes or until the vegetables are crisp-tender, stirring occasionally. Add broth, bulgur, and ⅓ cup of the water. Bring to boiling; reduce heat. Cover and simmer 10 to 12 minutes or until bulgur is tender and liquid is absorbed. Transfer to a large bowl and let cool 5 minutes, stirring occasionally.
3. In a small bowl whisk together eggs, coriander, salt, and pepper. Add egg mixture and ground turkey to bulgur mixture; mix well. Shape into 30 meatballs, about 2 Tbsp. each. Place on the prepared pan.
4. Bake meatballs 15 to 18 minutes or until done (165°F).
5. Meanwhile, in a large saucepan combine cranberry sauce, orange juice, cornstarch, cayenne, and the remaining 2 Tbsp. water. Cook about 5 minutes or until sauce is thickened and bubbly, stirring constantly. Add cooked meatballs to sauce, stirring gently to coat.

PER SERVING (3 meatballs each) **CAL** 197, **FAT** 7 g (2 g sat. fat), **CHOL** 79 mg, **SODIUM** 356 mg, **CARB** 20 g (2 g fiber, 11 g sugars), **PRO** 14 g

Basil-Parmesan Zucchini Roll-Ups

Basil-Parmesan Zucchini Roll-Ups

5g CARB

SERVES 10
TOTAL 30 min.

- 3 large zucchini, trimmed
- ¾ cup reduced-fat cream cheese (neufchatel), softened
- ½ cup coarsely torn fresh basil
- 1 4-oz. jar diced pimiento peppers, drained
- ⅓ cup grated Parmesan cheese
- 1 small clove garlic, minced
- 1½ tsp. Italian seasoning, crushed
- ½ tsp. black pepper

1. Using a vegetable peeler, slice zucchini into 30 very thin strips (about ¹⁄₁₆ inch thick) that run the full length and width. (Reserve any remaining zucchini for another use.) Lay the strips in a single layer on a clean work surface.
2. In a medium bowl stir together the remaining ingredients. Spread 2 tsp. of the mixture over each zucchini strip. Roll up strips. If necessary, secure with cocktail picks.

TIP To ensure zucchini strips are a uniform width and length, shave off several strips from one side and reserve for another use. Shave about 5 strips that are the full length and width of the zucchini, then flip the zucchini over and shave from the other side.

PER SERVING (3 roll-ups each) **CAL** 77, **FAT** 5 g (3 g sat. fat), **CHOL** 6 mg, **SODIUM** 132 mg, **CARB** 5 g (1 g fiber, 3 g sugars), **PRO** 4 g

Mini Sausage Stuffing Tarts

13g
CARB

SERVES 12
HANDS ON 30 min.
TOTAL 1 hr. 10 min.

- 4 oz. reduced-fat cream cheese (neufchatel), softened
- 2 eggs
- 3 Tbsp. canola oil
- ⅔ cup all-purpose flour
- ½ cup whole wheat pastry flour
- 8 oz. lean ground turkey sausage
- 1 cup chopped fresh mushrooms
- ½ cup chopped onion
- ⅓ cup chopped celery
- 1 slice whole wheat bread, dried and crumbled
- ¼ cup chopped dried tart cherries
- 1 tsp. dried rosemary or sage, crushed
- ½ cup water

1. Preheat oven to 375°F. Coat twenty-four 1¾-inch muffin cups with *nonstick cooking spray*.

2. In a large bowl beat cream cheese with a mixer on medium until smooth. Add one of the eggs and the oil; beat until well combined, scraping sides of bowl as needed. Add all-purpose flour and pastry flour; mix until just combined. Form dough into a ball and wrap in plastic wrap; refrigerate 30 minutes.

3. Meanwhile, in a large skillet cook sausage, mushrooms, onion, and celery over medium heat about 9 minutes or until sausage is browned and vegetables are tender, stirring occasionally. Remove from heat; stir in bread crumbs, cherries, and rosemary. In a small bowl whisk together the remaining egg and the water. Drizzle over sausage mixture; stir until combined.

4. Divide dough into 24 balls. Press balls evenly into bottoms and up sides of prepared muffin cups. Spoon the sausage mixture evenly into cups.

5. Bake 15 to 20 minutes or until filling is heated and crusts are golden brown on the edges. Let cool on a wire rack 5 minutes. Serve warm.

PER SERVING (2 tarts each) **CAL** 153,
FAT 8 g (2 g sat. fat), **CHOL** 46 mg,
SODIUM 221 mg, **CARB** 13 g (1 g fiber, 2 g sugars),
PRO 7 g

Pumpkin Coconut Nibbles

15g
CARB

SERVES 10
HANDS ON 20 min.
TOTAL 40 min.

- 1½ cups old-fashioned oats
- ½ cup chopped slivered almonds
- ⅓ cup unsweetened shredded coconut
- ¾ cup canned pumpkin
- 2 Tbsp. honey
- 2 tsp. pumpkin pie spice
- ¼ tsp. salt
- ⅛ tsp. cayenne pepper

1. Preheat oven to 300°F. Spread oats, almonds, and coconut in a large rimmed baking sheet. Bake 8 to 10 minutes or until lightly browned, stirring once or twice. Cool completely on a wire rack.

2. In a large bowl stir together the remaining ingredients. Stir in the toasted oat mixture.

3. Shape pumpkin mixture into 20 balls, about 2 tsp. each. Place the balls on a serving tray. Serve immediately.

TO STORE Place balls in an airtight container. Store in the refrigerator up to 2 days.

PER SERVING (2 balls each) **CAL** 114,
FAT 5 g (2 g sat. fat), **CHOL** 0 mg, **SODIUM** 104 mg,
CARB 15 g (3 g fiber, 5 g sugars), **PRO** 3 g

Mini
Sausage
Stuffing
Tarts

QUICK TIP

To dry and crumble one slice of bread, let the bread dry out overnight or bake in a 300°F oven about 8 minutes or until dried. Crumble with your hands or in a food processor.

Pumpkin
Coconut
Nibbles

Parmesan-
Crusted
Brussels
Sprouts

Parmesan-Crusted Brussels Sprouts

10g **CARB**

SERVES 8
HANDS ON 35 min.
TOTAL 55 min.

- 1 lb. Brussels sprouts, trimmed, halved if large
- 2 eggs
- ⅔ cup whole wheat panko
- ⅓ cup grated Parmesan cheese
- ½ tsp. garlic powder
- ½ tsp. salt
- ¼ tsp. black pepper
  Nonstick cooking spray
- 1 cup prepared marinara sauce (optional)

1. Preheat oven to 425°F. Line a 15×10-inch baking pan with parchment paper.
2. In a 4-qt. pot fitted with a steamer basket bring 2 inches of water to boiling. Add Brussels sprouts; cover and steam 5 to 7 minutes or until tender. Transfer to a paper towel-lined plate and pat dry.
3. In a shallow dish lightly beat eggs. In another shallow dish stir together panko, Parmesan, garlic powder, salt, and pepper. Roll each sprout in egg to coat. Allow excess to drip off, then roll in the panko mixture to coat. Place sprouts in the prepared baking pan with space between them. Coat the sprouts lightly with cooking spray.
4. Bake 15 to 18 minutes or until golden brown and tender, turning once. If desired, serve with marinara sauce.

TIP If you are using large Brussels sprouts, you may need to use 2 large rimmed baking sheets to avoid crowding the pans. Bake as directed in Step 4, switching the pan positions in oven halfway through.

PER SERVING (about ½ cup each) **CAL** 80, **FAT** 2 g (1 g sat. fat), **CHOL** 49 mg, **SODIUM** 245 mg, **CARB** 10 g (3 g fiber, 1 g sugars), **PRO** 5 g

Avocado-Stuffed Mushrooms

Avocado-Stuffed Mushrooms

3g **CARB**

SERVES 12
HANDS ON 20 min.
TOTAL 30 min.

- 1 lb. button and/or cremini mushrooms with 2-inch caps (about 12 mushrooms)
- 5 Tbsp. olive oil
- 3 Tbsp. champagne vinegar
- 2 Tbsp. chopped red onion
- 1 tsp. kosher salt
- ⅓ cup chopped toasted hazelnuts or almonds
- 1 Tbsp. chopped fresh rosemary
- 1 avocado, halved, seeded, peeled and chopped

1. Preheat oven to 400°F. Remove stems from mushrooms. Place stems and caps in a 15×10-inch baking pan. Drizzle with 3 Tbsp. of the olive oil; toss to coat. Bake 10 to 12 minutes or until just tender; cool. Lightly pat mushrooms with a paper towel to dry excess moisture.
2. In a medium bowl combine vinegar, onion, and salt. Finely chop mushroom stems; add to vinegar mixture along with nuts, rosemary, avocado, and the remaining 2 Tbsp. olive oil. Spoon avocado mixture into mushroom caps.

TIP Any leftover filling can be enjoyed on whole grain crackers.

PER SERVING (1 stuffed mushroom each) **CAL** 99, **FAT** 9 g (1 g sat. fat), **CHOL** 0 mg, **SODIUM** 163 mg, **CARB** 3 g (1 g fiber, 1 g sugars), **PRO** 2 g

Crispy
Buttercup
Squash
Poppers

Crispy Buttercup Squash Poppers

19g
CARB

SERVES 6
HANDS ON 40 min.
TOTAL 1 hr.

- 1 3- to 3½-lb. buttercup or butternut squash
- 2 eggs, lightly beaten
- 3 Tbsp. all-purpose flour
- ¾ cup panko
- ¼ cup grated Parmesan cheese
- ½ tsp. black pepper
   Nonstick olive oil cooking spray
- 1 lemon
- 1 5.3- to 6-oz. carton plain fat-free Greek yogurt
- ¼ cup light mayonnaise
- 1 clove garlic, minced
   Dash salt
   Dash ground chipotle chile pepper or chili powder (optional)
   Fresh arugula (optional)

1. Preheat oven to 425°. Line a 15×10-inch baking pan with foil. Halve, seed, and peel squash. Cut half of the squash into 3-inch strips. Reserve the remaining squash for another use.
2. In a shallow dish combine eggs and flour. In another shallow dish stir together panko, cheese, and black pepper. Roll squash strips in egg mixture, then in crumb mixture to coat. Place in the prepared baking pan.
3. Lightly coat tops of squash strips with cooking spray. Bake 20 to 25 minutes or until tender and golden.
4. Meanwhile, for sauce, remove ½ tsp. zest and squeeze 2 tsp. juice from lemon. In a small bowl combine lemon zest, 1 to 2 tsp. of the juice, and the next five ingredients (through ground chipotle pepper). If desired, sprinkle with additional chipotle pepper.
5. If desired, arrange squash poppers on a bed of arugula. Serve with sauce for dipping.

PER SERVING *(3 poppers + 2 Tbsp. sauce each)*
CAL 152, **FAT** 5 g *(1 g sat. fat)*, **CHOL** 68 mg, **SODIUM** 234 mg, **CARB** 19 g *(2 g fiber, 3 g sugars)*, **PRO** 8 g

Tahini-Yogurt Dip

4g
CARB

SERVES 4
TOTAL 10 min.

- 2 Tbsp. tahini
- 1 Tbsp. lemon juice, plus more to taste
- 1 clove garlic, minced
- ¼ tsp. salt
- 1 cup plain low-fat Greek yogurt
- ¼ cup chopped fresh cilantro
  Dippers: baby carrots, sliced radishes, or whole wheat pita wedges triangles.

. In a small bowl stir together tahini, lemon juice, garlic, and salt until smooth. Stir in yogurt and cilantro until combined. If desired, add more lemon juice to taste. Transfer dip to a serving bowl. Serve with desired dippers.

TIP If the tahini is very thick, you can use a food processor to help blend the dip. Place all ingredients except cilantro in the food processor and process until smooth. Add cilantro and pulse until well mixed.

PER SERVING (⅓ cup each) **CAL** 88, **FAT** 5 g (1 g sat. fat), **CHOL** 6 mg, **SODIUM** 168 mg, **CARB** 4 g (0 g fiber, 2 g sugars), **PRO** 7 g

Tahini-Yogurt Dip

Black Bean Dip

Parmesan Carrot Crisps

8g
CARB

SERVES	18
HANDS ON	15 min.
TOTAL	1 hr.

- 1½ cups whole wheat pastry flour
- 1 cup finely shredded Parmesan cheese or Gruyère cheese
- ¾ cup finely shredded carrots
- 2 Tbsp. chopped fresh thyme or 2 tsp. dried thyme, crushed
- 1 tsp. baking powder
- ⅛ tsp. salt
- ⅓ cup chilled butter, cut up
- ¼ cup water
- ⅛ tsp. freshly ground black pepper
  Apricot fruit spread or fig preserves (optional)

1. Preheat oven to 325°F. In a large bowl stir together the first six ingredients (through salt). Using a pastry blender, cut in butter until mixture resembled coarse crumbs and starts to stick together. Add the water. Stir just until combined. Gather dough into a ball and shape into a square.
2. Place dough square between two sheets of parchment paper. Roll dough to a 10-inch square about ⅛ inch thick. Remove top sheet of paper. Use your hands to reshape dough into a square if necessary. Transfer dough with parchment onto a baking sheet. Cut into long skinny sticks, about 1×5 inches each. Separate each stick. Sprinkle tops of sticks lightly with freshly ground pepper.
3. Bake 40 to 50 minutes or until evenly browned and centers are dry to the touch. Set on pan on a wire rack 5 minutes. Separate crisps and transfer to wire rack to cool completely. If desired, serve with fruit spread.

TO STORE Place crisps in an airtight container or resealable plastic bag. Store at room temperature up to 24 hours.

PER SERVING (1 crisp each) **CAL** 88,
FAT 5 g (3 g sat. fat), **CHOL** 12 mg,
SODIUM 149 mg, **CARB** 8 g (2 g fiber, 0 g sugars),
PRO 3 g

Black Bean Dip

17g
CARB

SERVES	4
TOTAL	10 min.

- 1 15-oz. can low-sodium black beans, rinsed and drained
- ¼ cup plain low-fat Greek yogurt
- 2 tsp. lime juice
- ½ tsp. ground cumin
- ½ tsp. dried oregano, crushed
- ½ tsp. garlic powder
- ¼ tsp. smoked paprika or sweet paprika
- ¼ tsp. salt
- ¼ tsp. black pepper
- ¼ tsp. cayenne pepper or ground chipotle pepper (optional)
- ¼ cup chopped fresh cilantro or green onions
- ¼ cup chopped onion
- 2 tsp. olive oil

1. Place the first nine ingredients (through black pepper) in a food processor or blender. Process about 20 seconds or until well combined. If desired, for a spicier dip, add cayenne (or ground chipotle) to taste, up to ¼ tsp. Add cilantro, onion, and oil. Pulse until well mixed, about 20 seconds. Transfer to a serving bowl.

TIP Serve this dip with red bell pepper pieces, zucchini slices, or whole grain tortilla chips.

PER SERVING (⅓ cup each) **CAL** 129,
FAT 3 g (1 g sat. fat), **CHOL** 1 mg, **SODIUM** 210 mg,
CARB 17 g (5 g fiber, 1 g sugars), **PRO** 7 g

Parmesan
Carrot Crisps

QUICK TIP

When cutting dough into sticks, use a pastry cutter with a crimped wheel to create a textured edge.

Pear Crostini with Blue Cheese Spread

Pear Crostini with Blue Cheese Spread

15g
CARB

SERVES 8
HANDS ON 20 min.
TOTAL 30 min.

- 6 oz. white or whole wheat baguette-style French bread, cut into 24 slices
  Nonstick olive oil cooking spray
- 2 oz. reduced-fat cream cheese (neufchatel), softened
- ¼ cup crumbled blue cheese (1 oz.)
- 3 Tbsp. light sour cream
- 2 cloves garlic, minced
- 1 medium pear, cut into 24 slices
- 1 Tbsp. balsamic glaze
- 1 tsp. chopped fresh thyme

1. Preheat oven to 400°F. Arrange bread slices on a large baking sheet and coat with cooking spray. Bake about 10 minutes or until golden. Transfer to a wire rack and let cool.
2. Meanwhile, in a medium bowl stir together cream cheese, blue cheese, sour cream, and garlic.
3. Spread cheese mixture on toasted bread slices and top with pear slices. Drizzle with balsamic glaze and top with thyme.

PER SERVING *(3 crostini each)* **CAL** 103, **FAT** 3 g *(2 g sat. fat)*, **CHOL** 9 mg, **SODIUM** 181 mg, **CARB** 15 g *(1 g fiber, 3 g sugars)*, **PRO** 3 g

Raspberry-Prosecco Cocktail

8g
CARB

SERVES 2
TOTAL 10 min.

- 1 Tbsp. framboise (raspberry eau de vie)
- 1 tsp. Campari
- 1 cup Prosecco or other sparkling wine, chilled
- 2 sugar cubes
  Fresh raspberries (optional)

1. For each drink, add 1½ tsp. of the framboise and ½ tsp. of the Campari to a champagne flute. Slowly pour in ½ cup of the Prosecco; stir gently. Add a sugar cube. If desired, serve with a wooden skewer threaded with raspberries.

PER SERVING *(4 oz. each)* **CAL** 109, **FAT** 0 g, **CHOL** 0 mg, **SODIUM** 0 mg, **CARB** 8 g *(0 g fiber, 4 g sugars)*, **PRO** 0 g

Raspberry-
Prosecco
Cocktail

Holiday
Champagne
Cocktails

Holiday Champagne Cocktails

6g | **SERVES** 8
CARB | **TOTAL** 10 min.

1 cup pomegranate, cranberry, blood orange, or regular orange juice, chilled
½ cup vodka, chilled
  Ice (optional)
2 cups champagne, chilled
  Optional garnishes: lime or orange slices, fresh rosemary or thyme sprigs, fresh cranberries, and/or pomegranate seeds

1. In a pitcher combine juice and vodka. If desired, add ice. Slowly pour in champagne; stir gently. Garnish servings as desired.

PER SERVING (½ cup each) **CAL** 91, **FAT** 0 g, **CHOL** 0 mg, **SODIUM** 3 mg, **CARB** 6 g (0 g fiber, 4 g sugars), **PRO** 1 g

Spiked Cinnamon-Cider Iced Tea

8g | **SERVES** 8
CARB | **HANDS ON** 10 min.
       | **TOTAL** 15 min.

3 cups water
3 black tea bags
2 3-inch cinnamon sticks
2 cups apple cider
1 cup bourbon
  Cinnamon sticks (optional)
  Thinly sliced apples

1. In a 3-qt. saucepan bring water just to boiling; remove from heat. Add tea bags and two 2 cinnamon sticks. Cover; let steep 5 minutes. Remove and discard tea bags, pressing out any liquid with a spoon. Add apple cider and bourbon; heat through. Remove and discard cinnamon sticks. Cover and refrigerate.
2. If desired, garnish each serving with an additional cinnamon stick and apple slices.

TIP For a nonalcoholic version, increase the apple cider to 2¾ cups and add ¼ cup lemon juice.

TIP Tea may also be served warm.

PER SERVING (¾ cup each) **CAL** 98, **FAT** 0 g, **CHOL** 0 mg, **SODIUM** 11 mg, **CARB** 8 g (0 g fiber, 7 g sugars), **PRO** 0 g

Spiked
Cinnamon-
Cider Iced
Tea

3

COMFORTING
SOUPS & STEWS

Whether it's a sledding party, after-shopping
meal, or Friday supper, warm soup will
satisfy everyone. This versatile dish simmers
patiently in a slow cooker or on the stove top
as diners make their way to the table.
Best of all, the veggie-full bowls keep you on
a healthful track during the busy holidays.

50

59

63

**Farro and Beef
Stew with
Roasted Winter
Vegetables**

4. Stir farro into meat mixture. Cook 30 to 35 minutes more or until farro is tender. Stir in roasted vegetables. If desired, stir in parsley before serving.

TIP If using regular barley or wheat berries, cook about 45 minutes more or until tender.

TO MAKE AHEAD Prepare as directed through Step 4. Cool slightly. Transfer to an airtight container. Cover and chill up to 3 days or freeze up to 2 months. To serve, thaw stew in the refrigerator 1 to 2 days if frozen. Transfer thawed or chilled stew to a Dutch oven. Cook over medium until boiling, stirring occasionally. If necessary, stir in additional beef broth to reach desired consistency.

PER SERVING *(1⅓ cups each)* **CAL** 406, **FAT** 13 g *(3 g sat. fat)*, **CHOL** 62 mg, **SODIUM** 566 mg, **CARB** 36 g *(4 g fiber, 3 g sugars)*, **PRO** 27 g

Steak and Lentil Soup

25g
CARB

SERVES 6
HANDS ON 25 min.
SLOW COOK 7 hr.

- 1 lb. boneless beef sirloin steak, trimmed and cut into ¾-inch pieces
- 4 cups 50%-less-sodium beef broth
- 1 cup French lentils, rinsed and drained
- 1 cup water
- ¾ cup coarsely chopped red bell pepper
- ½ cup chopped onion
- ½ cup sliced carrot
- ½ cup sliced celery
- 2 cloves garlic, minced
- 1 tsp. ground cumin
- ½ tsp. salt
- ¼ tsp. cayenne pepper
- ⅓ cup chopped fresh parsley

1. If desired, in a large nonstick skillet cook and stir meat over medium-high until browned. Place meat in a 3½- or 4-qt. slow cooker. Stir in the next 11 ingredients (through cayenne pepper).
2. Cover and cook on low 7 to 8 hours or high 3½ to 4 hours. Stir in parsley.

PER SERVING *(1⅓ cups each)* **CAL** 240, **FAT** 4 g *(1 g sat. fat)*, **CHOL** 52 mg, **SODIUM** 530 mg, **CARB** 25 g *(5 g fiber, 3 g sugars)*, **PRO** 27 g

Farro and Beef Stew with Roasted Winter Vegetables

36g
CARB

SERVES 6
HANDS ON 30 min.
TOTAL 2 hr. 35 min.

- ¼ cup all-purpose flour
- ½ tsp. salt
- ½ tsp. black pepper
- 2 to 2½ lb. boneless beef chuck roast, trimmed and cut into 1-inch pieces
- ¼ cup olive oil
- ½ cup chopped onion
- 2 cloves garlic, minced
- ½ tsp. dried thyme, crushed
- 1 14.5-oz. can beef broth
- 2 cups water
- 1 cup dry red wine
- 4 red or yellow potatoes and/or sweet potatoes, cut into 1-inch pieces
- 4 carrots and/or parsnips, peeled and cut into 1-inch pieces
- ½ cup farro, regular barley, or wheat berries
- 2 Tbsp. chopped fresh parsley (optional)

1. In a plastic bag combine flour and ¼ tsp. each of the salt and pepper. Add meat pieces, a few at a time, shaking to coat. In a Dutch oven heat 1 Tbsp. of the oil over medium-high. Add half of the meat; cook until browned. Remove from pan. Repeat with another 1 Tbsp. of the oil and the remaining meat.
2. Add onion, garlic, and thyme to a 4- to 5-qt. Dutch oven. Cook and stir 3 minutes. Drain off fat. Return all of the meat to pan. Add broth, stirring to scrape up any browned bits from pan. Stir in the water and wine. Bring to boiling; reduce heat. Cover and simmer 1 hour.
3. Meanwhile, preheat oven to 375°F. In a shallow roasting pan combine potatoes and carrots and/or parsnips. Drizzle with the remaining 2 Tbsp. oil; sprinkle with the remaining ¼ tsp. each salt and pepper. Toss to coat. Roast, uncovered, 35 to 45 minutes or until vegetables are tender and light brown, stirring once or twice.

Steak and
Lentil Soup

Spanish-Style Beef Stew

17g CARB

SERVES 8
HANDS ON 25 min.
TOTAL 1 hr. 5 min.

- 1½ lb. boneless beef chuck roast, trimmed and cut into 1-inch pieces
- 1 to 2 Tbsp. olive oil
- 1 14.5-oz. can 50%-less-sodium beef broth
- 1 28-oz. can fire-roasted diced tomatoes, undrained
- 12 oz. tiny red new potatoes, halved if large
- 2 cups coarsely chopped red and/or green bell peppers
- 1 medium onion, cut into wedges
- 1 cup dry red wine
- 2 tsp. dried oregano, crushed
- 1 tsp. smoked paprika
- 1 orange
- ⅓ cup sliced pitted green olives
- ¼ cup chopped fresh parsley

1. Use a 6-qt. electric or stove-top pressure cooker. For electric cooker, use sauté setting to cook meat, half at a time, in 1 Tbsp. oil until browned, adding additional oil if needed; for stove-top cooker, cook meat, half at a time, directly in the pot in 1 Tbsp. oil over medium-high until browned, adding additional oil if needed. Remove meat.

2. Add broth to electric or stove-top cooker. Bring to simmering, stirring to scrape up any browned bits from bottom. Return meat. Stir in next seven ingredients (through paprika).

3. Lock lid in place. Set electric cooker on high pressure to cook 15 minutes. For stove-top cooker, bring up to pressure over medium-high according to manufacturer's directions; reduce heat enough to maintain steady (but not excessive) pressure. Cook 15 minutes. Remove from heat.

4. For electric and stove-top models, let stand to release pressure naturally, at least 15 minutes or according to manufacturer's directions. If necessary, quickly release any remaining pressure according to manufacturer's directions. Open lid carefully.

5. Remove 1 tsp. zest and squeeze 2 Tbsp. juice from orange. Add orange zest and juice to meat mixture. Stir in olives and parsley.

PER SERVING (1 ½ cups each) **CAL** 241, **FAT** 8 g *(3 g sat. fat)*, **CHOL** 59 mg, **SODIUM** 487 mg, **CARB** 17 g *(3 g fiber, 7 g sugars)*, **PRO** 20 g

Spanish-Style Beef Stew

Hearty
Pork-Beer
Stew

Hearty Pork-Beer Stew

27g CARB

SERVES 8
HANDS ON 35 min.
SLOW COOK 7 hr.

Nonstick cooking spray
1 lb. boneless pork shoulder, trimmed and cut into ¾-inch pieces
2 large sweet potatoes, peeled and cut into 1-inch pieces
3 medium parsnips, peeled and cut into ¾-inch pieces
2 small green apples, cored and cut into wedges
1 medium onion, cut into thin wedges
3 cups vegetable broth
1 Tbsp. packed brown sugar
1 Tbsp. Dijon-style mustard
1½ tsp. dried thyme, crushed
2 cloves garlic, minced
½ tsp. crushed red pepper
1 12-oz. can beer or 1½ cups vegetable broth
4 large roma tomatoes, cut up

1. Lightly coat a large skillet with cooking spray; heat over medium-high. Add meat; cook and stir until browned. Drain off fat.
2. In a 5- to 6-qt. slow cooker combine sweet potatoes, parsnips, apples, and onion. Top with meat. In a small bowl combine ½ cup of the broth and next five ingredients (through crushed red pepper); pour over mixture in cooker. Add remaining 2½ cups broth and the beer.
3. Cover and cook on low 7 to 8 hours or high 3½ to 4 hours. Stir in tomatoes.

PER SERVING *(1 cup each)* **CAL** 209,
FAT 4 g *(1 g sat. fat)*, **CHOL** 37 mg,
SODIUM 471 mg, **CARB** 27 g *(5 g fiber, 12 g sugars)*, **PRO** 14 g

Basque
Chicken
Stew

Chicken Goulash with Peas and Caraway

36g CARB

SERVES 8
HANDS ON 35 min.
SLOW COOK 8 hr.

- 1 Tbsp. sweet Hungarian paprika
- ½ tsp. salt
- ¼ tsp. black pepper
- 2½ lb. bone-in chicken thighs, skin removed
- 2 medium red bell peppers, cut into 1-inch pieces
- 2 cups quartered and thinly sliced sweet onion
- 1 15-oz. can tomato sauce
- 1 14.5-oz. can diced tomatoes, undrained
- 1 cup sliced carrots
- 2 cloves garlic, minced
- ½ tsp. caraway seeds, crushed
- 1 cup reduced-sodium chicken broth
- 1 cup frozen peas
- 1 Tbsp. cider vinegar
- 4 cups hot cooked noodles

1. In a small bowl stir together paprika, salt, and black pepper. Sprinkle spice mixture over chicken; rub in with your fingers.
2. In a 5- to 6-qt. slow cooker combine the next seven ingredients (through caraway seeds). Top with chicken; add broth to cooker. Cover and cook on low 8 hours or high 4 hours.
3. Turn off cooker. Remove chicken and shred using two forks; discard bones. Stir shredded chicken, frozen peas, and vinegar into mixture in cooker. Let stand, covered, 10 minutes. Serve over noodles.

PER SERVING *(1 cup each)* **CAL** 312,
FAT 6 g *(2 g sat. fat)*, **CHOL** 123 mg,
SODIUM 716 mg, **CARB** 36 g *(6 g fiber, 8 g sugars)*,
PRO 28 g

Basque Chicken Stew

16g CARB

SERVES 6
HANDS ON 15 min.
TOTAL 35 min.

- 1¼ lb. skinless, boneless chicken thighs, cut into 2-inch pieces
- ½ tsp. salt
- ¼ tsp. black pepper
- 1 Tbsp. olive oil
- 1 onion, thinly sliced
- 1 red bell pepper, cut into ¼-inch-thick strips
- 2 cloves garlic, minced
- 1 14.5-oz. can diced tomatoes, drained
- 1 cup chicken broth
- ¾ lb. red potatoes, cut into ½-inch wedges
- ½ tsp. dried savory, crushed
- 1 tsp. fresh snipped thyme or ¼ tsp. dried thyme, crushed
- ⅓ cup small pimiento-stuffed olives (optional)

1. Season chicken with ¼ tsp. of the salt and the black pepper. In a 5- to 6-qt. Dutch oven heat oil over medium-high. Add chicken; cook about 2 minutes per side or until lightly browned.
2. Add onion and bell pepper; cook about 3 minutes or until crisp-tender. Add garlic; cook and stir 30 seconds more. Add the next five ingredients (through thyme) and the remaining ¼ tsp. salt. Bring to boiling; reduce heat. Cover and simmer about 20 minutes or until chicken and potatoes are tender. Remove from heat. Stir in olives and, if desired, garnish with additional fresh thyme.

SLOW COOKER DIRECTIONS In a 3½- or 4-qt. slow cooker combine chicken, potatoes, bell pepper, and onion. Stir in tomatoes, broth, garlic, thyme, salt, and black pepper. Cover and cook on low 10 to 11 hours or on high for 5 to 5½ hours. Stir in olives and, if desired, garnish with additional fresh thyme.

PER SERVING *(1½ cups each)* **CAL** 204,
FAT 6 g *(1 g sat. fat)*, **CHOL** 79 mg,
SODIUM 576 mg, **CARB** 16 g *(3 g fiber, 5 g sugars)*,
PRO 21 g

Chicken
Goulash with
Peas and
Caraway

New
World
Chili

New World Chili

35g CARB

SERVES 6
TOTAL 45 min.

- 1 lb. turkey breast tenderloin, cut into 1-inch pieces
- 1 28-oz. can no-salt-added diced tomatoes, undrained
- 1 15-oz. can no-salt-added black beans, rinsed and drained
- 1 8-oz. can no-salt-added tomato sauce
- 1 cup ¾-inch pieces butternut squash or pumpkin
- ½ cup chopped onion
- ¾ cup chicken broth
- ½ cup frozen whole kernel corn
- ½ cup dried cranberries
- 1 fresh jalapeño chile pepper, halved, seeded, and finely chopped (tip, *p. 154*)
- 1 Tbsp. chili powder
- 1 clove garlic, minced
- 2 cups shredded fresh spinach (optional)
  Shredded Monterey Jack cheese with jalapeño peppers (optional)

1. In a 4- to 5-qt. Dutch oven combine the first 12 ingredients (through garlic). Bring to boiling; reduce heat. Simmer, covered, about 15 minutes or until squash is tender. If desired, just before serving stir in spinach and sprinkle individual servings with cheese.

PER SERVING (1⅓ cups each) **CAL** 239, **FAT** 1 g (0 g sat. fat), **CHOL** 47 mg, **SODIUM** 256 mg, **CARB** 35 g (8 g fiber, 15 g sugars), **PRO** 25 g

Southwest Salmon Chowder

Southwest Salmon Chowder

25g CARB

SERVES 8
HANDS ON 35 min.
TOTAL 50 min.

- 1½ lb. fresh or frozen skinless salmon fillets or three 6- to 7.5-oz. cans skinless, boneless salmon, drained and flaked
- 1½ cups water
- 2 Tbsp. olive oil
- ¾ cup chopped red or orange bell pepper
- ¼ cup thinly sliced green onions (white and green parts separated)
- 3 Tbsp. all-purpose flour
- 3½ cups reduced-sodium vegetable broth
- 3 cups ½-inch pieces red-skin potatoes
- 2½ cups low-fat (1%) milk
- ½ tsp. salt
- ½ tsp. black pepper
- ¼ to ½ tsp. ground ancho chile pepper or chili powder
- 2 cups frozen whole kernel corn, thawed
- 1 tsp. lime zest
  Chopped avocado and/or lime wedges (optional)

1. Thaw salmon, if frozen. To poach fillets, in a large skillet bring the water to boiling. Add fillets. Return to boiling; reduce heat. Cover and simmer 6 to 8 minutes or until salmon flakes easily. Remove from skillet, discarding liquid. Flake salmon into ½-inch pieces (if using canned salmon, skip this step and omit the water).

2. In a 6-qt. Dutch oven heat oil over medium-high. Add bell pepper and white parts of onions; cook and stir about 3 minutes or just until tender. Stir in flour; cook and stir 1 minute.

3. Gradually stir in broth. Add potatoes, milk, salt, black pepper, and ground ancho pepper. Bring to boiling; reduce heat. Cover and simmer about 15 minutes or until slightly thick and vegetables are tender, stirring occasionally. Add corn; cook and stir 2 minutes more. Gently stir in poached or canned salmon and lime zest; heat through.

4. Top servings with green parts of onions and, if desired, avocado, lime wedges, and/or additional ground ancho pepper.

TO MAKE AHEAD Transfer cooled soup to a freezer container; cover. Freeze up to 3 months. To serve, thaw in refrigerator overnight. Reheat in a covered Dutch oven over low, stirring occasionally.

PER SERVING (1¼ cups each) **CAL** 280, **FAT** 10 g (2 g sat. fat), **CHOL** 51 mg, **SODIUM** 287 mg, **CARB** 25 g (3 g fiber, 8 g sugars), **PRO** 22 g

Kohlrabi, Potato, and Leek Soup

32g
CARB

SERVES 8

TOTAL 1 hr.

- 1 15-oz. can chickpeas, rinsed and drained
- 4 Tbsp. olive oil
- ½ tsp. garlic powder
- ½ tsp. onion powder
- 2 lb. leeks, white and light green parts only, halved lengthwise and sliced ½ inch thick
- 3 cloves garlic, minced
- 1 Tbsp. chopped fresh rosemary or 1 tsp. dried rosemary, crushed
- 2½ cups no-salt-added chicken broth or vegetable broth
- 2½ cups water
- 1 bay leaf
- 1 lb. russet potatoes, peeled and finely chopped
- 1 lb. kohlrabi, peeled and finely chopped
- 1 Tbsp. cider vinegar
- 1 tsp. salt
  Black pepper

1. Preheat oven to 350°F. Pat chickpeas dry. Spread evenly in a rimmed baking pan. Bake 45 to 50 minutes or until crisp all the way through, stirring occasionally. Transfer chickpeas to a bowl. Add 1 Tbsp. of the oil, the garlic powder, and onion powder; toss to coat.
2. Meanwhile, in a 4- to 5-qt. pot heat 2 Tbsp. of the oil over medium. Add leeks; cover and cook about 15 minutes or until softened.
3. Add garlic and rosemary; cook and stir 1 minute. Add the next five ingredients (through kohlrabi). Bring to boiling; reduce heat. Cover and simmer 15 to 20 minutes or until potatoes and kohlrabi are tender. Remove from heat.
4. Discard bay leaf and let soup cool slightly. Stir in the remaining 1 Tbsp. oil, the vinegar, and salt. Working in batches, transfer soup to blender; cover and blend until smooth. Return to pot. Season with pepper.
5. Top each serving with 2 Tbsp. of the crispy chickpeas. If desired, garnish with additional fresh rosemary.

PER SERVING *(1 cup each)* **CAL** 225,
FAT 8 g *(1 g sat. fat)*, **CHOL** 0 mg, **SODIUM** 463 mg,
CARB 32 g *(6 g fiber, 5 g sugars)*, **PRO** 7 g

Slow Cooker Minestrone

Slow Cooker Minestrone

42g
CARB

SERVES 8
HANDS ON 30 min.
SLOW COOK 6 hr. 15 min.

- 6 cups no-salt-added vegetable broth
- 2 15-oz. cans no-salt-added red kidney beans, rinsed and drained
- 2 15-oz. cans no-salt-added diced tomatoes, undrained
- 2 cups sliced carrots
- 2 cups fresh green beans, trimmed and cut into 2-inch pieces
- 1½ cups chopped celery
- ½ cup chopped red onion
- 2 Tbsp. dried Italian seasoning, crushed
- 3 cloves garlic, minced
- 1 tsp. crushed red pepper
- ¾ tsp. salt
- ½ tsp. black pepper
- 2 cups sliced halved zucchini
- 1 cup dried whole wheat pasta elbows or other small pasta (4 oz.)
- ½ cup freshly grated Parmesan cheese

1. In a 6- to 8-qt. slow cooker combine the first 10 ingredients (through crushed red pepper), ¼ tsp. of the salt, and the black pepper. Cover and cook on low 6 to 8 hours.

2. Stir in zucchini, pasta, and the remaining ½ tsp. salt. Cover and cook on low 15 to 20 minutes or until pasta is tender. Serve immediately. Sprinkle individual servings with Parmesan.

PER SERVING *(2 cups each)* **CAL** 222,
FAT 2 g *(1 g sat. fat)*, **CHOL** 4 mg, **SODIUM** 525 mg,
CARB 42 g *(13 g fiber, 10 g sugars)*, **PRO** 12 g

Gingered
Carrot-
Sweet Potato
Soup

Gingered Carrot-Sweet Potato Soup

30g
CARB

SERVES 6
TOTAL 30 min.

- 1 lb. carrots, peeled and thinly sliced
- 1 large sweet potato, peeled and cut into ½-inch cubes
- 3 14.5-oz. cans reduced-sodium vegetable broth
- 1 tsp. ground ginger
- 1 19-oz. can no-salt-added cannellini beans, rinsed and drained
- ¼ salt
- ¼ tsp. black pepper
- ½ cup low-fat sour cream or crème fraîche (optional)
- 2 Tbsp. snipped fresh chives or sliced green onion (optional)

1. In a 4-qt. Dutch oven combine carrots, sweet potato, broth, and ginger. Bring to boiling; reduce heat. Cover and simmer 10 to 12 minutes or until vegetables are tender. Cool slightly.

2. In a blender combine one-fourth of the carrot mixture and one-fourth of the beans; cover and blend until smooth, removing cap from blender lid and holding a folded kitchen towel over opening in lid. Repeat with the remaining carrot mixture and beans,

one-fourth at a time. Return all of the soup to Dutch oven. Heat through. Stir in salt and pepper.

3. If desired, in a bowl stir together sour cream and chives. Spoon onto individual servings of soup and sprinkle with additional snipped chives and ground ginger.

TIP Substitute russet potatoes for the carrots and sweet potato and ground cumin for the ground ginger.

TO MAKE AHEAD Prepare soup as directed; let cool. Transfer soup to an airtight container; cover. Freeze up to 3 months. Thaw and reheat in the microwave or on the stove top.

PER SERVING *(1½ cups each)* **CAL** 144,
FAT 1 g *(0 g sat. fat)*, **CHOL** 0 mg, **SODIUM** 314 mg,
CARB 30 g *(7 g fiber, 8 g sugars)*, **PRO** 5 g

Curried
Sweet
Potato and
Peanut
Soup

Curried Sweet Potato and Peanut Soup

37g
CARB

SERVES 6
HANDS ON 35 min.
TOTAL 40 min.

- 2 Tbsp. canola oil
- 1½ cups diced yellow onion
- 1 Tbsp. minced garlic
- 1 Tbsp. minced fresh ginger
- 4 tsp. red curry paste
- 1 fresh serrano chile, seeded and finely chopped (tip, *p. 154*)
- 1 lb. sweet potatoes, peeled and cubed (½-inch pieces)
- 3 cups water
- 1 cup canned unsweetened light coconut milk
- ¾ cup unsalted dry-roasted peanuts
- 1 15-oz. can cannellini beans, rinsed and drained
- ¾ tsp. salt
- ¼ tsp. black pepper
- ¼ cup chopped fresh cilantro
- 2 Tbsp. lime juice
- ¼ cup unsalted roasted pumpkin seeds (pepitas)
  Lime wedges

1. In a 4- to 5-qt. pot heat oil over medium-high. Add onion; cook about 4 minutes or until tender, stirring frequently.
2. Stir in garlic, ginger, curry paste, and serrano chile; cook and stir 1 minute. Stir in sweet potatoes and the water. Bring to boiling; reduce heat. Simmer, partially covered, 10 to 12 minutes or until sweet potatoes are tender. Cool slightly.
3. Transfer half of the soup to a blender; add coconut milk and peanuts. Cover and blend until smooth. Return to pot with the remaining soup. Stir in beans, salt, and pepper; heat through. Remove from heat. Stir in cilantro and lime juice. Serve with pumpkin seeds, additional cilantro, and lime wedges.

TIP You can find red curry paste in small glass jars in the Asian section of many grocery stores.

PER SERVING (1 cup each) **CAL** 345,
FAT 19 g (4 g sat. fat), **CHOL** 0 mg,
SODIUM 594 mg, **CARB** 37 g (8 g fiber, 7 g sugars),
PRO 13 g

Black Bean and Vegetable Soup with Prosciutto Gremolata

39g
CARB

SERVES 6
TOTAL 30 min.

- 1 Tbsp. olive oil
- ½ of a 14.4-oz. pkg. (2 cups) frozen bell pepper and onion stir-fry vegetables
- 1 32-oz. carton reduced-sodium chicken broth
- 2 15-oz. cans no-salt-added black beans, rinsed and drained
- 1 10-oz. sweet potato, peeled and cut into ½-inch pieces
- 1 14.5-oz. can no-salt-added fire-roasted diced tomatoes, undrained
- 2 tsp. hot chili powder or berbere seasoning
- ¼ tsp. black pepper
- 1 recipe Prosciutto Gremolata

1. In a 4-qt. Dutch oven heat oil over medium-high. Add frozen vegetables; cook 3 minutes, stirring occasionally. Stir in next five ingredients (through chili powder).
2. Bring to boiling; reduce heat. Cover and simmer about 15 minutes or until sweet potato is tender, stirring occasionally. Stir in pepper. Top servings with Prosciutto Gremolata.

PROSCIUTTO GREMOLATA Place 2 thin slices prosciutto between paper towels and place on a plate. Microwave 1 minute; cool and crumble. In a small bowl combine prosciutto, ¼ cup snipped fresh parsley, 2 tsp. lemon zest, and 1 clove garlic, minced.

PER SERVING (1½ cups each) **CAL** 230,
FAT 3 g (0 g sat. fat), **CHOL** 1 mg, **SODIUM** 769 mg,
CARB 39 g (9 g fiber, 6 g sugars), **PRO** 12 g

Black Bean
and Vegetable
Soup with
Prosciutto
Gremolata

Broccoli-Potato Soup

29g CARB | **SERVES** 6
HANDS ON 30 min.
SLOW COOK 5 hr.

- 5 cups peeled and chopped baking potatoes
- 1 32-oz. carton reduced-sodium chicken broth
- 1 cup chopped carrots
- 1 cup chopped onion
- 1 to 2 tsp. curry powder
- 5 cups broccoli florets
- 1 cup half-and-half
- ¼ tsp. salt
- ¼ tsp. black pepper
  Toppings: plain low-fat Greek yogurt, sliced green onions, shredded sharp cheddar cheese, crumbled crisp-cooked bacon, and/or rye bread croutons (optional)

1. In a 5- to 6-qt. slow cooker combine potatoes, broth, carrots, onion, and curry powder. Cover and cook on low 5 to 6 hours or high 2½ to 3 hours. If slow cooker is on low, turn to high. Stir in broccoli. Cover and cook 30 minutes more.

2. Using an immersion blender, blend vegetable mixture as desired until slightly chunky or smooth. (Or cool slightly and, working in batches, transfer to a food processor or blender; cover and process or blend as desired. Return to cooker.)

3. Stir in half-and-half, salt, and pepper. Cover and cook on high 10 minutes more to blend flavors. Serve with desired toppings.

PER SERVING (1 ½ cups each) **CAL** 178, **FAT** 5 g (3 g sat. fat), **CHOL** 14 mg, **SODIUM** 518 mg, **CARB** 29 g (5 g fiber, 6 g sugars), **PRO** 8 g

Butternut Squash–Cannellini Bean Soup

24g
CARB

SERVES 8
HANDS ON 30 min.
TOTAL 1 hr.

2 Tbsp. olive oil
1 medium onion, very thinly sliced
3 cloves garlic, minced
2 15-oz. cans no-salt-added cannellini beans, rinsed and drained

1½ to 2 lb. butternut squash, peeled, seeded, and cut into 1-inch cubes (about 3½ cups)
1½ cups halved cherry or grape tomatoes
4 cups reduced-sodium chicken broth
3 cups water
1½ tsp. chopped fresh rosemary
½ tsp. salt
¼ tsp. cracked black pepper

1. In a 4- to 5-qt. Dutch oven heat oil over medium-high. Add onion; cook and stir 7 to 8 minutes or until golden. Add garlic; cook and stir 1 minute. Add the remaining ingredients. Bring to boiling; reduce heat. Cover and simmer about 30 minutes or until squash is tender, stirring occasionally.

PER SERVING (1¼ cups each) **CAL** 157, **FAT** 4 g (1 g sat. fat), **CHOL** 0 mg, **SODIUM** 460 mg, **CARB** 24 g (6 g fiber, 4 g sugars), **PRO** 7 g

Roasted Red Pepper Bisque with Orange Gremolata

24g CARB

SERVES 6
HANDS ON 20 min.
SLOW COOK 5 hr.

- 6 large red bell peppers
- 1½ cups peeled and chopped sweet potato
- 1 cup fresh or frozen whole kernel corn
- ½ cup coarsely chopped onion
- 2 tsp. paprika
- 2 cloves garlic, sliced
- 4 cups reduced-sodium chicken or vegetable broth
- ¼ tsp. salt
- ¼ tsp. cayenne pepper
- 1 recipe Orange Gremolata *(right)*

1. Preheat oven to 425°F. Cut bell peppers lengthwise into quarters; remove stems, seeds, and membranes. Place pepper quarters, cut sides down, on a foil-lined baking sheet. Roast about 20 minutes or until peppers are charred and very tender. Bring foil up around peppers and fold edges together to enclose. Let stand until cool enough to handle. Peel off and discard skins. Coarsely chop peppers.
2. In a 3½- or 4-qt. slow cooker combine peppers and the next five ingredients (through garlic). Add broth. Cover and cook on low 5 to 6 hours or high 2½ to 3 hours.
3. Using an immersion blender, blend vegetable mixture until smooth. (Or working in batches, cool slightly and transfer to a blender or food processor. Cover and blend or process until smooth. Return to cooker.) Stir in salt and cayenne pepper.
4. Top servings with Orange Gremolata.

PER SERVING *(1 cup each)* **CAL** 119, **FAT** 1 g *(0 g sat. fat)*, **CHOL** 0 mg, **SODIUM** 497 mg, **CARB** 24 g *(5 g fiber, 10 g sugars)*, **PRO** 5 g

ORANGE GREMOLATA

In a small bowl stir together ¼ cup chopped fresh Italian parsley, 1 tsp. orange zest, and 1 clove garlic, minced.

4

MAIN-DISH
MASTERPIECES

Festive dinners call for a main-dish
centerpiece that feeds a crowd with style.
Choices include fancy stuffed pork, braised
pot roast, comforting pot pie, and
baked pasta. Each brings a new twist to
traditions that's designed to delight. These
nutrition superstars prove you don't have
to sacrifice flavor to eat healthfully.

Kale, Cranberry, and Bulgar Salad with Turkey

Spinach-Artichoke Turkey Noodle Casserole

29g CARB

SERVES 6
HANDS ON 15 min.
TOTAL 30 min.

Nonstick cooking spray
- 3 cups dried wide whole wheat egg noodles
- 1 Tbsp. canola oil
- 1 to 1¼ lb. extra-lean ground turkey breast
- 1¼ cups thinly sliced red bell pepper
- 1 cup chopped onion
- 4 cloves garlic, minced
- 4 oz. fat-free cream cheese, cubed
- 1 cup reduced-sodium chicken broth
- ⅓ cup light mayonnaise
- ¼ tsp. crushed red pepper
- ¼ tsp. black pepper
- 1 9-oz. pkg. frozen chopped spinach, thawed
- 1 9-oz. pkg. frozen artichoke hearts or chopped broccoli, thawed
- ½ cup finely shredded Parmesan cheese (2 oz.)
- 2 Tbsp. chopped fresh chives or ¼ cup chopped fresh parsley

1. Preheat oven to 350°F. Coat a 3-qt. rectangular or square baking dish with cooking spray. Cook noodles according to package directions; drain.
2. Meanwhile, in a large nonstick skillet heat oil over medium. Add ground turkey, bell pepper, onion, and garlic; cook until turkey is no longer pink. Remove from heat. Stir in cream cheese until melted.
3. In a large bowl whisk together broth, mayonnaise, crushed red pepper, and black pepper. Wrap spinach and artichokes in a double layer of paper towels and blot dry. Add spinach and artichokes to mayonnaise mixture. Stir in turkey mixture, noodles, and Parmesan cheese. Transfer to the prepared baking dish.
4. Bake 15 minutes. Stir turkey mixture. Bake 10 to 15 minutes more or until heated through. Sprinkle with chives.

PER SERVING (1½ cups each) **CAL** 288,
FAT 7 g (2 g sat. fat), **CHOL** 44 mg,
SODIUM 415 mg, **CARB** 29 g (7 g fiber, 4 g sugars),
PRO 29 g

Kale, Cranberry, and Bulgur Salad with Turkey

46g CARB

SERVES 4
HANDS ON 45 min.
TOTAL 1 hr. 30 min.

- ¾ cup red bulgur
- 2 Tbsp. sliced almonds
- 1 lb. turkey breast cutlets
- ¾ tsp. salt
- ¾ tsp. black pepper
- 3½ Tbsp. olive oil
- 2 Tbsp. cider vinegar
- 1 Tbsp. pure maple syrup
- 1 tsp. Dijon-style mustard
- 4 cups finely chopped fresh kale, stems removed
- 1 Fuji apple, chopped
- ½ cup finely chopped shallot
- ¼ cup dried cranberries

1. Cook bulgur according to package directions.
2. Meanwhile, in a large skillet toast almonds over medium 3 to 4 minutes or until golden and fragrant, stirring frequently. Remove from pan.

3. Sprinkle both sides of turkey cutlets with ¼ tsp. each of the salt and pepper. In the same skillet heat 1½ tsp. of the oil over medium-high. Cook cutlets in hot oil about 4 minutes or until lightly browned and cooked through, turning once,. Transfer to a cutting board and cut into 1-inch pieces.
4. In a large bowl whisk together the remaining 3 Tbsp. oil, the vinegar, maple syrup, mustard, and the remaining ½ tsp. each salt and pepper. Add kale, apple, shallot, cranberries, cooked bulgur, and turkey; toss to combine. Chill 30 minutes or until ready to serve. Sprinkle with the toasted almonds.

TIP Red bulgur is made from red wheat and has a rich, dark brown color. Look for Bob's Red Mill brand at the supermarket. You can substitute any variety of bulgur for the red.

PER SERVING (2½ cups each) **CAL** 450,
FAT 16 g (3 g sat. fat), **CHOL** 71 mg,
SODIUM 572 mg, **CARB** 46 g (5 g fiber, 10 g sugars), **PRO** 33 g

Spinach-
Artichoke
Turkey Noodle
Casserole

QUICK TIP

You can find delicata and acorn squash in the produce section of many grocery stores. Delicata squash has an edible rind. Acorn squash does not. You can remove the rind of acorn squash before serving or simply eat around it.

Roasted Chicken and Winter Squash over Mixed Greens

Roasted Chicken and Winter Squash over Mixed Greens

39g
CARB

SERVES 4
HANDS ON 25 min.
TOTAL 45 min.

Nonstick cooking spray
2½ lb. delicata squash or acorn squash
1 lemon
3 Tbsp. olive oil
2 Tbsp. whole-grain mustard
3 cloves garlic, minced
1 Tbsp. chopped fresh rosemary or 1 tsp. dried rosemary, crushed
1 tsp. black pepper
½ tsp. salt
1 lb. boneless, skinless chicken breast
1 Tbsp. pure maple syrup
1½ tsp. fresh thyme leaves
8 cups mixed salad greens
4 tsp. grated Parmesan cheese
4 tsp. salted roasted pumpkin seeds

1. Preheat oven to 425°F. Coat a large rimmed baking pan with cooking spray.
2. Cut squash in half lengthwise and remove seeds. Cut crosswise into 1-inch slices.
3. Remove 1 tsp. zest and squeeze 2 Tbsp. juice from lemon. In a large bowl combine zest and 1½ tsp. of the juice with 1 Tbsp. of the olive oil, 1½ Tbsp. of the mustard, the garlic, rosemary, ½ tsp. of the pepper, and ¼ tsp. of the salt. Add squash slices and chicken; stir to coat. Arrange in a single layer in the prepared pan.
4. Bake, without turning, 20 to 22 minutes or until squash starts to brown and chicken is done (165°F). Transfer chicken to a cutting board and slice.
5. Meanwhile, in a medium bowl whisk together the remaining 2 Tbsp. olive oil, 1½ tsp. mustard, 1½ Tbsp. lemon juice, the maple syrup, thyme, and the remaining ½ tsp. pepper and ¼ tsp. salt. Add greens; toss to coat.
6. Arrange greens on serving plates. Top with the chicken and squash, Parmesan, and pumpkin seeds.

PER SERVING *(2 cups salad + 3 oz. chicken + 4 oz. squash each)* **CAL** 415, **FAT** 17 g *(3 g sat. fat)*, **CHOL** 84 mg, **SODIUM** 566 mg, **CARB** 39 g *(7 g fiber, 10 g sugars)*, **PRO** 31 g

Alfredo Chicken and Cauliflower Rice Bake

Alfredo Chicken and Cauliflower Rice Bake

11g
CARB

SERVES 6
HANDS ON 20 min.
TOTAL 50 min.

5 cups small cauliflower florets
1 tsp. dried basil, crushed
¼ tsp. black pepper
2½ cups fresh baby spinach
2 cups chopped cooked chicken breast
1½ cups light Alfredo pasta sauce
2 Tbsp. grated Parmesan cheese
½ cup panko
1 Tbsp. olive oil

1. Preheat oven to 400°F. Working in batches, place cauliflower in a food processor. Cover and pulse until crumbly and mixture resembles the texture of rice.
2. Transfer cauliflower "rice" to a 3-qt. casserole dish. Sprinkle with basil and pepper; toss to coat. Bake 15 minutes.
3. Stir in spinach, chicken, and Alfredo sauce. Sprinkle with cheese. Combine panko and oil; sprinkle over cauliflower mixture. Bake 20 to 25 minutes more or until top is brown.

PER SERVING *(1 cup each)* **CAL** 195, **FAT** 8 g *(3 g sat. fat)*, **CHOL** 61 mg, **SODIUM** 454 mg, **CARB** 11 g *(2 g fiber, 3 g sugars)*, **PRO** 18 g

Chicken and Brussels Sprout Salad with Bacon Vinaigrette

Apricot-Garlic Glazed Drumsticks with Roasted Green Beans and Fingerlings

41g CARB

SERVES 4
HANDS ON 25 min.
TOTAL 1 hr.

- 1 lb. multicolor fingerling potatoes, halved lengthwise
- 1 lb. thin green beans, trimmed
- 1 cup halved and thinly sliced red onion
- 2 Tbsp. olive oil
- ¾ tsp. kosher salt
- ¼ tsp. black pepper
- 1 orange
- 3 Tbsp. apricot preserves
- 1 Tbsp. reduced-sodium soy sauce
- 3 cloves garlic, minced
  Dash black pepper
- 4 large chicken drumsticks (1½ to 2 lb.), skinned

1. Preheat oven to 425°F. Place potatoes in a large microwave-safe bowl. Cover and microwave 2 minutes.
2. In a 15×10-inch baking pan combine potatoes, green beans, and onion. Drizzle with oil and sprinkle with ½ tsp. of the salt and the ¼ tsp. pepper.
3. For glaze, remove ½ tsp. zest and squeeze 2 Tbsp. juice from orange. In a small bowl combine orange zest and juice, apricot preserves, soy sauce, garlic, dash pepper, and the remaining ¼ tsp. salt. Nestle chicken into vegetables and brush chicken with half of the glaze.
4. Roast 15 minutes. Remove from oven. Stir vegetables; turn chicken and brush with the remaining glaze. Roast about 20 minutes more or until chicken is done (at least 175°F) and potatoes are tender.

PER SERVING (1 drumstick + 1½ cups vegetables each) **CAL** 328, **FAT** 10 g (2 g sat. fat), **CHOL** 60 mg, **SODIUM** 432 mg, **CARB** 41 g (7 g fiber, 14 g sugars), **PRO** 20 g

Chicken and Brussels Sprout Salad with Bacon Vinaigrette

28g CARB

SERVES 4
TOTAL 40 min.

- 4 slices center-cut bacon (1 oz.)
- 2 Tbsp. olive oil
- ¼ cup finely chopped shallot
- 2 Tbsp. red wine vinegar
- 1 tsp. honey
- ½ tsp. Dijon-style mustard
- ½ tsp. salt
- ½ tsp. black pepper
- 1 lb. Brussels sprouts, trimmed and shredded (6 cups)
- 2 medium Fuji apples, cored and thinly sliced
- 2 cups shredded cooked chicken breast (12 oz.)

1. In a large nonstick skillet cook bacon over medium 5 to 7 minutes or until crisp. Drain on a paper towel-lined plate. Coarsely crumble.
2. Drain all but 1 Tbsp. drippings from pan. Add oil to pan; heat over medium. Add shallot; cook and stir 1 to 2 minutes or until tender and light brown. Remove from heat.
3. Add vinegar, honey, mustard, salt, and pepper to pan; whisk to combine. Add Brussels sprouts; toss to coat. Cook 2 to 3 minutes or until slightly wilted, tossing occasionally.
4. In a large bowl combine apples and chicken. Add Brussels sprouts and any liquid from pan; toss gently to combine. Top with reserved bacon.

TIP To shred Brussels sprouts, first cut off any woody stems. Halve sprouts lengthwise, then slice crosswise or use a food processor fitted with a slicing blade. Separate into shreds. To simplify, purchase sliced Brussels sprouts from the produce section.

PER SERVING (2 cups each) **CAL** 357, **FAT** 12 g (3 g sat. fat), **CHOL** 75 mg, **SODIUM** 514 mg, **CARB** 28 g (7 g fiber, 16 g sugars), **PRO** 34 g

Apricot-Garlic Glazed Drumsticks with Roasted Green Beans and Fingerlings

Chicken Pot Pie with Cauliflower-Parmesan Topping

22g CARB

SERVES 6	
HANDS ON 25 min.	
TOTAL 1 hr. 15 min.	

- 2 **cups shredded cooked chicken breast**
- 1 **10.8-oz. pkg. frozen lightly seasoned garlic baby peas and mushrooms**
- 1 **10.75-oz. can reduced-fat and reduced-sodium condensed cream of mushroom soup**
- 1 **cup frozen whole kernel corn**
- 1 **cup sliced celery**
- ½ **cup chopped onion**
- 3 **Tbsp. chopped fresh parsley**
- 2 **tsp. chopped fresh thyme**
- 1 **tsp. lemon zest**
- ¼ **tsp. black pepper**
- 1 **10-oz. pkg. frozen riced cauliflower**
- ⅓ **cup grated Parmesan cheese**
- ¼ **cup panko or all-purpose flour**
- 2 **Tbsp. unsalted butter, melted**

1. Preheat oven to 425°F. In a large bowl combine the first 10 ingredients (through pepper). Transfer to a 9-inch deep-dish pie plate, spreading evenly.
2. For topping, in a medium bowl stir together cauliflower, Parmesan, panko, and melted butter. Sprinkle over chicken mixture.
3. Bake about 40 minutes or until filling is heated through and topping is golden. Let stand 10 minutes before serving. Sprinkle with additional parsley.

PER SERVING (1 ⅓ cups each) **CAL** 259, **FAT** 9 g (4 g sat. fat), **CHOL** 56 mg, **SODIUM** 627 mg, **CARB** 22 g (4 g fiber, 7 g sugars), **PRO** 21 g

Stuffed
Pork
Tenderloin
with Wild
Rice

Stuffed Pork Tenderloin with Wild Rice

33g CARB

SERVES 2
HANDS ON 30 min.
TOTAL 1 hr.

- ¼ cup dried cranberries
- 8 oz. boneless pork tenderloin, trimmed
- ½ cup chopped apple
- ½ cup cooked wild rice
- 1 tsp. chopped fresh thyme
- 1 tsp. chopped fresh rosemary
- 1 tsp. chopped fresh parsley
- ¼ tsp. salt
- ¼ tsp. black pepper
- 2 cups green beans, trimmed

1. Preheat oven to 450°F. Line a 15×10-inch baking pan with foil.

2. In a small bowl combine ½ cup boiling water and the cranberries. Cover and let stand 10 minutes. Drain.

3. Butterfly the meat by making a lengthwise cut down the center of the meat, cutting to within ½ inch of the other side; spread open. Place knife in the "V" of the cut and cut horizontally to the cut surface and away from the center cut to within ½ inch of the other side of the meat. Repeat on opposite side of the "V." Spread meat open. Use the heel of your hand to gently flatten the meat to an even thickness.

4. Stir the apple and rice into the drained cranberries. Add ½ tsp. each thyme, rosemary, and parsley and ⅛ tsp. each of the salt and pepper.

5. Spread half of the rice mixture across the flattened pork, leaving a 1-inch border all around. Starting on a long side, tightly roll the pork, securing with a few toothpicks. Sprinkle with the remaining ½ tsp. each thyme, rosemary, and parsley, and ⅛ tsp. salt and pepper. Place stuffed pork in the prepared baking pan.

6. Roast 20 to 25 minutes or until the internal temperature reaches 145°F. Remove from oven. Let pork rest 3 minutes.

7. Meanwhile, place a steamer basket in a 2-qt. saucepan. Add water to just below the basket and bring to boiling. Add beans to basket; cover. Reduce heat to medium and steam 3 to 5 minutes or until tender. In a medium nonstick skillet cook remaining rice mixture over medium until heated through.

8. Slice pork crosswise into thick rounds. Serve with beans and rice mixture. If desired, sprinkle with additional thyme and pepper.

PER SERVING *(3 slices pork + ¼ cup wild rice mixture + ½ cup green beans each)* **CAL** 302, **FAT** 7 g *(2 g sat. fat)*, **CHOL** 62 mg, **SODIUM** 334 mg, **CARB** 33 g *(3 g fiber, 18 g sugars)*, **PRO** 27 g

Arugula Salad with Roasted Pork, Pears, and Blue Cheese

Arugula Salad with Roasted Pork, Pears, and Blue Cheese

25g CARB

SERVES 4
HANDS ON 25 min.
TOTAL 50 min.

- 2 Tbsp. chopped walnuts
- 3 Tbsp. balsamic vinegar
- 2 Tbsp. olive oil
- 2 tsp. lemon juice
- 1 tsp. honey
- 1 tsp. Dijon-style mustard
- 2 tsp. finely chopped fresh rosemary or ¾ tsp. dried rosemary
- 1 clove garlic, minced
- ½ tsp. salt
- ½ tsp. black pepper
- 1 lb. pork tenderloin
- 8 cups fresh arugula
- 4 small or 2 large red pears, cut into wedges
- ¼ cup crumbled blue cheese (1 oz.)

1. Preheat oven to 400°F. Coat a large rimmed baking sheet with *nonstick cooking spray.*

2. In a medium skillet cook walnuts over medium until golden, stirring frequently.

3. For dressing, in a large bowl whisk together the next seven ingredients (through garlic) and ¼ tsp. each of the salt and pepper. Place pork on the prepared baking sheet. Brush with 1 Tbsp. of the dressing and sprinkle with the remaining ¼ tsp. each salt and pepper.

4. Roast 20 to 22 minutes or until meat registers 145°F. Transfer pork to a cutting board; let stand 5 minutes. Cut into ¾-inch-thick slices.

5. Add arugula and pears to dressing in large bowl; toss to coat. Divide among plates. Top with pork, cheese, and toasted walnuts.

PER SERVING *(3 cups salad + 3 oz. pork each)* **CAL** 352, **FAT** 16 g *(4 g sat. fat)*, **CHOL** 62 mg, **SODIUM** 692 mg, **CARB** 25 g *(5 g fiber, 16 g sugars)*, **PRO** 27 g

Grilled
Pork Loin
with Spicy
Apricot
Chutney

Grilled Pork Loin with Spicy Apricot Chutney

24g
CARB

SERVES 6
HANDS ON 25 min.
TOTAL 9 hr. 40 min.

- 1 1½-lb. boneless pork top loin roast (single loin), trimmed of fat
- ½ cup lemon juice
- ¼ cup honey
- 2 Tbsp. olive oil
- 2 tsp. Dijon-style mustard
- 4 cloves garlic, minced
- ¾ tsp. kosher salt
- 6 fresh apricots, pitted and quartered, or 2 fresh peaches, pitted and coarsely chopped
- 6 Tbsp. chopped red onion
- 5 Tbsp. packed brown sugar
- 2 fresh jalapeño chile peppers, seeded (if desired) and finely chopped (tip, p. 154)
- 2 Tbsp. white wine vinegar
- 2 Tbsp. lemon juice
- 1 Tbsp. honey
- 3 cloves garlic, minced
- ¼ tsp. kosher salt
- ¼ tsp. black pepper
   Fresh cilantro leaves

1. Place meat in a resealable plastic bag set in a shallow dish. For marinade, in a small bowl whisk together the ½ cup lemon juice, ¼ cup honey, 1 Tbsp. of the oil, the mustard, 4 cloves garlic, and ¾ tsp. salt. Pour marinade over meat. Seal bag; turn to coat meat. Marinate in the refrigerator 8 to 24 hours, turning occasionally.
2. Drain meat, discarding marinade. Brush meat with the remaining 1 Tbsp. oil.
3. Prepare grill for indirect heat using a drip pan. Place meat on greased rack over drip pan. Grill, covered, over indirect medium heat 1¼ to 1½ hours or until meat registers 145°F, turning once. Transfer meat to cutting board; let stand 3 minutes.
4. Meanwhile, for chutney, in a medium saucepan combine the next 10 ingredients (through black pepper). Bring to boiling; reduce heat. Cover and simmer 5 minutes. Simmer, uncovered, about 10 minutes more or until slightly thickened.
5. Serve meat with chutney and sprinkle with cilantro.

PER SERVING (3½ oz. meat + ⅓ cup chutney each) CAL 268, **FAT** 7 g (2 g sat. fat), **CHOL** 71 mg, **SODIUM** 172 mg, **CARB** 24 g (1 g fiber, 21 g sugars), **PRO** 26 g

Garlic and Herb Roast Pork and Vegetables

40g
CARB

SERVES 4
HANDS ON 30 min.
TOTAL 1 hr. 15 min.

- 4 5- to 6-oz. russet potatoes
- 2 Tbsp. canola oil
- ¾ tsp. salt
- 1 2½- to 2¾-lb. boneless pork top loin roast (single loin), trimmed
- 2 tsp. salt-free garlic-and-herb seasoning
   Nonstick cooking spray
- 6 medium carrots, peeled, quartered lengthwise, and cut into 2-inch pieces
- 8 oz. Brussels sprouts, trimmed and halved (if large)
- 1 large onion, cut into 1-inch wedges
- ½ tsp. black pepper
   Chopped fresh chives (optional)

1. Arrange oven racks in top one-third and bottom one-third of oven. Preheat oven to 425°F. Prick potatoes with a fork. Brush with 1 Tbsp. of the oil and sprinkle with ¼ tsp. of the salt. Wrap each potato in foil.
2. Sprinkle meat with garlic-and-herb seasoning. Coat a large ovenproof skillet with cooking spray; heat over medium-high. Add meat and cook about 4 minutes or until browned on both sides. Transfer skillet to top oven rack. Place potatoes on rack next to skillet. Roast 25 minutes.
3. Meanwhile, line a 15×10-inch baking pan with foil; coat with cooking spray. In a large bowl combine carrots, Brussels sprouts, and onion. Drizzle with the remaining 1 Tbsp. oil and sprinkle with pepper and the remaining ½ tsp. salt; toss to coat. Spread vegetables in the prepared pan. Transfer pan to bottom oven rack. Roast 25 to 30 minutes or until meat registers 145°F, potatoes are fork-tender, and roasted vegetables are tender and brown.
4. Transfer meat to a cutting board; let stand 5 minutes. Serve half of the meat with potatoes and roasted vegetables, drizzling with pan juices and topping with chives if desired. Reserve remaining meat for another use.

PER SERVING (4 oz. meat + 1 potato + 1 cup roasted vegetables each) CAL 422, **FAT** 13 g (2 g sat. fat), **CHOL** 89 mg, **SODIUM** 593 mg, **CARB** 40 g (9 g fiber, 9 g sugars), **PRO** 37 g

TO STORE

Place remaining meat in an airtight container and store in refrigerator up to 3 days or freeze up to 3 months.

Garlic and Herb Roast Pork and Vegetables

**Garlic-Rosemary Roast Beef
with Horseradish Sauce**

2g
CARB

SERVES 8
HANDS ON 50 min.
TOTAL 1 hr.

- 3 lb. boneless beef eye of round
  roast
- 1 tsp. salt
- ¾ tsp. black pepper
- 1 Tbsp. vegetable oil
- 3 Tbsp. unsalted butter, softened
- ¼ cup finely chopped shallots
- 2 Tbsp. finely chopped fresh
  rosemary
- 3 cloves garlic, finely chopped
- 1 cup plain nonfat Greek yogurt
- 1 Tbsp. prepared horseradish
- 1 tsp. Dijon-style mustard
- 1 tsp. lemon juice
- 1 clove garlic, grated

1. Preheat oven to 400°F. Sprinkle
roast with ¾ tsp. of the salt and ½ tsp.
of the pepper. In a large ovenproof
skillet heat oil over medium-high.
Add roast; cook about 10 minutes or
until browned on all sides, turning
occasionally. Remove from heat.
2. In a bowl stir together butter,
shallots, rosemary, and finely chopped
garlic; spread over roast. Transfer pan
to oven. Roast 35 to 40 minutes or until
meat registers 135°F for medium-rare.
Transfer roast to a cutting board; let
rest 10 minutes.
3. Meanwhile, for horseradish sauce,
in a small bowl whisk together the
remaining ingredients. Stir in the
remaining ¼ tsp. each salt and pepper.
Thinly slice beef and serve with sauce.

TIP If you don't have a large ovenproof
skillet, brown the roast in a large
skillet and transfer it to a roasting pan
for Step 2.

PER SERVING *(3 oz. beef + 2 Tbsp. sauce each)*
CAL 359, **FAT** 20 g *(8 g sat. fat)*, **CHOL** 129 mg,
SODIUM 417 mg, **CARB** 2 g *(0 g fiber, 1 g sugars)*,
PRO 40 g

Coffee-Braised Pot Roast

24g
CARB

SERVES 8
HANDS ON 30 min.
TOTAL 3 hr.

- 1 3- to 3½-lb. beef chuck pot roast,
  trimmed of fat
- ½ tsp. salt
- ½ tsp. black pepper
- 1 Tbsp. vegetable oil
- 1 large onion, halved and sliced
- 1 medium green bell pepper, cut
  into 2-inch pieces
- 3 cloves garlic, minced
- ¾ cup 50%-less-sodium beef broth
- 1 8-oz. can crushed pineapple
  (juice pack), undrained
- 1 Tbsp. instant espresso or French
  roast coffee powder
- ¼ tsp. crushed red pepper
- ¼ tsp. ground allspice
- 2 lb. sweet potatoes, peeled,
  halved lengthwise, and cut into
  2-inch pieces

1. Preheat oven to 325°F. Sprinkle roast
with salt and black pepper. In a 6-qt.
Dutch oven heat oil over medium-high.
Add roast; cook until browned on all
sides. Remove meat from oven.
2. Add onion, bell pepper, and garlic
to Dutch oven. Cook and stir 4 to
5 minutes or until onion and garlic are
tender and starting to brown. Return
meat to Dutch oven. Add the next five
ingredients (through allspice). Bring to
boiling. Cover pot and transfer to oven.
3. Roast 1¾ hours. Add sweet potatoes.
Roast, covered, about 45 minutes
more or until meat and vegetables are
tender. Transfer meat and vegetables
to a platter; cover to keep warm.
4. For sauce, bring liquid in Dutch
oven to boiling; reduce heat. Simmer,
uncovered, 10 to 15 minutes or until
slightly thickened. Serve meat and
vegetables with sauce. If desired,
sprinkle with additional crushed red
pepper.

PER SERVING *(3¾ oz. meat + ¼ cup sauce each)*
CAL 345, **FAT** 9 g *(3 g sat. fat)*, **CHOL** 111 mg,
SODIUM 364 mg, **CARB** 24 g *(3 g fiber, 9 g sugars)*,
PRO 40 g

Garlic-
Rosemary
Roast
Beef with
Horseradish
Sauce

Coffee-
Braised Pot
Roast

Flank Steak Salad with Arugula and Oranges

Skillet Steak with Mushroom Sauce

16g CARB

SERVES 4
HANDS ON 20 min.
TOTAL 25 min.

- 12 oz. boneless beef top sirloin steak, cut 1 inch thick and trimmed
- 2 tsp. salt-free steak grilling seasoning, such as Mrs. Dash
- 2 tsp. canola oil
- 6 oz. broccoli rabe, trimmed
- 2 cups frozen peas
- 3 cups sliced fresh mushrooms
- 1 cup no-salt-added beef broth
- 1 Tbsp. whole-grain mustard
- 2 tsp. cornstarch
- ¼ tsp. salt

1. Preheat oven to 350°F. Sprinkle steak with steak seasoning. In an extra-large cast-iron skillet heat oil over medium-high. Add steak and broccoli rabe. Cook 4 minutes, turning broccoli rabe once (do not turn steak). Place peas around steak. Transfer skillet to oven and bake about 8 minutes or until steak is medium-rare (145°F). Remove steak and vegetables from skillet; cover and keep warm.
2. For sauce, add mushrooms to drippings in skillet. Cook over medium-high 3 minutes, stirring occasionally. Whisk together the remaining ingredients; stir into mushrooms. Cook and stir until thick and bubbly. Cook and stir 1 minute more. Slice steak and serving with vegetables and sauce.

PER SERVING *(2½ oz. meat + ⅓ cup sauce each)* **CAL** 226, **FAT** 6 g *(2 g sat. fat)*, **CHOL** 51 mg, **SODIUM** 356 mg, **CARB** 16 g *(5 g fiber, 6 g sugars)*, **PRO** 26 g

Flank Steak Salad with Arugula and Oranges

22g CARB

SERVES 4
HANDS ON 20 min.
TOTAL 35 min.

- 8 oz. beef flank steak
- ½ tsp. kosher salt
- ½ tsp. black pepper
- 3 tsp. olive oil
- 4 navel oranges
- 1½ Tbsp. white wine vinegar
- 1½ tsp. honey
- 1 clove garlic, minced
- 1 tsp. Dijon-style mustard
- ½ tsp. smoked paprika
- ½ tsp. chopped fresh rosemary
- 1 5-oz. pkg. fresh baby arugula
- ½ cup very thinly sliced red onion
- 1 oz. goat cheese (chèvre) or feta, crumbled
- ¼ cup chopped pecans, toasted

1. Sprinkle both sides of steak with ¼ teaspoon each of the salt and pepper.
2. In a medium skillet heat 1 tsp. of the oil over medium-high. Add steak; cook 6 to 8 minutes per side or to desired doneness (145°F for medium). Cover lightly with foil; let stand 10 minutes.
3. Meanwhile, for vinaigrette, remove 1 tsp. zest and squeeze ¼ cup juice from one of the oranges. Peel the remaining three oranges and slice crosswise into rounds. In a bowl whisk together orange zest and juice, the remaining 2 tsp. oil, the vinegar, honey, garlic, mustard, paprika, rosemary, and the remaining ¼ tsp. each salt and pepper.
4. Slice steak thinly across the grain Arrange arugula on a platter or plates; top with orange slices, red onion, steak, goat cheese, and pecans. Drizzle with vinaigrette.

PER SERVING *(2½ cups each)* **CAL** 280, **FAT** 14 g *(4 g sat. fat)*, **CHOL** 45 mg, **SODIUM** 242 mg, **CARB** 22 g *(5 g fiber, 16 g sugars)*, **PRO** 17 g

Skillet
Steak with
Mushroom
Sauce

Warm Farro Salad with Salmon, Mushrooms, and Sweet Potatoes

Warm Farro Salad with Salmon, Mushrooms, and Sweet Potatoes

39g
CARB

SERVES 4
TOTAL 40 min.

Nonstick cooking spray
- 1½ cups water
- ¾ cup farro
- ¾ tsp. salt
- 8 oz. mixed fresh mushrooms, such as cremini, shiitake, and/or oyster, thickly sliced
- 1 medium sweet potato (8 oz.), cut into ½-inch pieces
- 4 Tbsp. olive oil
- 2 cloves garlic, minced
- ½ tsp. crushed red pepper
- 4 4-oz. salmon fillets, about 1 inch thick
- 2 Tbsp. white balsamic vinegar or white wine vinegar
- 2 tsp. lemon juice
- 1 tsp. honey
- 1 tsp. Dijon-style mustard
- ½ tsp. black pepper
- ½ cup thinly sliced shallot
- ⅓ cup chopped fresh sage or 1 Tbsp. dried sage, crushed

1. Preheat oven to 450°F. Coat a 15×10-inch baking pan with cooking spray.
2. In a 2-qt. saucepan combine the water, farro, and ¼ tsp. of the salt. Bring to boiling; stir and reduce heat. Cook, uncovered, 15 to 20 minutes or until farro is tender.
3. Meanwhile, in a large bowl combine mushrooms, sweet potato, 1 Tbsp. of the oil, half of the garlic, and ¼ tsp. each of the crushed red pepper and salt. Transfer to the prepared baking pan. Roast about 15 minutes or until vegetables are almost tender, stirring once.
4. Rub salmon with the remaining garlic and ¼ tsp. each salt and crushed red pepper. Nestle the salmon into the vegetables. Roast 6 to 8 minutes more or until sweet potato is tender and salmon just starts to flake.
5. In a large bowl whisk together the remaining 3 Tbsp. oil, the vinegar, lemon juice, honey, mustard, and pepper. Add the farro, roasted vegetables, shallot, and sage; toss to

combine. Divide among plates. Top with salmon. If desired, garnish with additional fresh sage.

PER SERVING *(1 cup salad + 4 oz. salmon + 2 Tbsp. dressing each)* **CAL** 542, **FAT** 31 g *(6 g sat. fat)*, **CHOL** 62 mg, **SODIUM** 535 mg, **CARB** 39 g *(5 g fiber, 7 g sugars)*, **PRO** 30 g

Hazelnut-Parsley Roast Tilapia

Hazelnut-Parsley Roast Tilapia

3g
CARB

SERVES 4
HANDS ON 20 min.
TOTAL 30 min.

- 4 5-oz. fresh or frozen tilapia fillets
- 2 Tbsp. olive oil
- ⅓ cup finely chopped hazelnuts
- ¼ cup chopped fresh parsley
- 1 small shallot, minced
- 2 tsp. lemon zest
- ⅛ tsp. salt
- ¼ tsp. black pepper
- 1½ Tbsp. lemon juice
- ¼ tsp. salt

1. Thaw fish, if frozen. Preheat oven to 450°F. Line a large rimmed baking sheet with foil; brush with 1 Tbsp. of the oil. Bring fish to room temperature by letting it stand on the counter 15 minutes.
2. Meanwhile, in a small bowl stir together hazelnuts, parsley, shallot, lemon zest, 1 tsp. of the oil, the ⅛ tsp. salt, and ⅛ tsp. of the pepper.
3. Pat both sides of fish dry with a paper towel. Place fish on the prepared baking sheet. Brush both sides of fish with lemon juice and the remaining 2 tsp. oil. Season fish with the ¼ tsp. salt and the remaining ⅛ tsp. pepper. Spoon hazelnut mixture over fish and pat gently to adhere.
4. Roast 7 to 10 minutes or until fish flakes easily. Serve immediately.

PER SERVING *(4 oz. fish each)* **CAL** 262, **FAT** 15 g *(2 g sat. fat)*, **CHOL** 71 mg, **SODIUM** 295 mg, **CARB** 3 g *(1 g fiber, 1 g sugars)*, **PRO** 30 g

Garlic-Oregano Roasted Salmon and Brussels Sprouts

Garlic-Oregano Roasted Salmon and Brussels Sprouts

11g
CARB

SERVES 6
HANDS ON 20 min.
TOTAL 45 min.

- 14 medium to large cloves garlic
- ¼ cup olive oil
- 2 Tbsp. chopped fresh oregano and/or thyme
- 1 tsp. salt
- ¾ tsp. black pepper
- 1¼ lb. Brussels sprouts, trimmed and sliced and/or quartered
- 2 lb. fresh salmon fillet, skin removed and cut into 6 portions
- ½ cup dry white wine
  Lemon wedges
  Freshly cracked black pepper

1. Preheat oven to 450°F. Mince two of the garlic cloves; halve the remaining 12 garlic cloves. In a small bowl combine minced garlic, oil, 1 Tbsp. of the oregano, ½ tsp. of the salt, and ¼ tsp. of the pepper. Place Brussels sprouts in a large roasting pan. Add halved garlic and 3 Tbsp. of the oil mixture; toss to coat. Roast 15 minutes, stirring once.
2. Meanwhile, brush salmon with the remaining oil mixture and sprinkle with the remaining ½ tsp. each salt and pepper.
3. Stir Brussels sprouts and drizzle with wine. Top with salmon. Roast 10 to 15 minutes more or just until salmon flakes. Top with the remaining 1 Tbsp. oregano. Serve with lemon wedges and freshly cracked black pepper.

PER SERVING *(4 oz. salmon + ¾ cup sprouts each)*
CAL 368, **FAT** 19 g *(3 g sat. fat)*, **CHOL** 83 mg,
SODIUM 477 mg, **CARB** 11 g *(3 g fiber, 2 g sugars)*,
PRO 33 g

Pan-Seard
Five-Spice
Scallops

Pan-Seared Five-Spice Scallops

9g
CARB

SERVES 4
TOTAL 20 min.

- 1 lb. fresh or frozen sea scallops
- 2 Tbsp. all-purpose flour
- 1 tsp. Chinese five-spice powder
  Dash cayenne pepper
- 1 Tbsp. sesame oil (not toasted) or peanut oil
- 1 10-oz. pkg. fresh baby spinach or kale
- 3 Tbsp. finely chopped cooked ham or cooked bacon pieces
- 1 Tbsp. water
- 2 Tbsp. seasoned rice vinegar
  Toasted sesame seeds (optional)

1. Thaw scallops, if frozen. In a resealable plastic bag combine flour, five-spice powder, and cayenne pepper. Add scallops; seal bag and shake to coat.
2. In a large skillet heat oil over medium. Add scallops; cook 3 to 5 minutes or until browned and opaque, turning once. Remove scallops from pan.
3. Add spinach and ham to skillet; sprinkle with the water. Cook, covered, over medium-high about 2 minutes or until spinach starts to wilt. Drizzle with vinegar, toss to coat. Return scallops to skillet; heat through. If desired, sprinkle with sesame seeds.

PER SERVING *(3 scallops + ⅔ cup spinach mixture each)* **CAL** 173, **FAT** 5 g *(1 g sat. fat)*, **CHOL** 41 mg, **SODIUM** 327 mg, **CARB** 9 g *(2 g fiber, 0 g sugars)*, **PRO** 22 g

White
Beans and
Tomatoes
with Kale
Pesto

Spanish Shrimp and Scallop Sauté

33g CARB | SERVES 4
TOTAL 25 min.

- 16 fresh or frozen medium shrimp (8 oz.), peeled and deveined (tails on if desired)
- 8 fresh or frozen sea scallops (8 oz.)
- 1 Tbsp. all-purpose flour
- 2 tsp. smoked paprika
- ¼ tsp. sugar
- ¼ tsp. black pepper
- ⅛ to ¼ tsp. cayenne pepper
- ¼ tsp. salt
- 2 Tbsp. butter
- 6 cloves garlic, thinly sliced
- 1 cup grape or cherry tomatoes, halved
- ¼ cup no-salt-added chicken broth
- 3 Tbsp. dry vermouth or dry white wine
- 1 Tbsp. fresh lemon juice
- 3 Tbsp. chopped fresh Italian parsley
- 3 Tbsp. chopped fresh chives
- 2 cups hot cooked brown rice

1. Thaw shrimp and scallops, if frozen. Halve scallops horizontally.
2. In a large resealable plastic bag combine the next five ingredients (through cayenne pepper) and ¼ tsp. of the salt. Add shrimp and scallops to the bag. Seal bag; shake to coat shrimp and scallops.
3. In a large nonstick skillet melt 1 Tbsp. of the butter over medium-high. Add garlic and the remaining ¼ tsp. salt; cook and stir 30 seconds. Add shrimp and scallops to the pan in an even layer; cook 2 minutes. Stir in the next four ingredients (through lemon juice); cook 2 to 3 minutes or until shrimp and scallops are opaque, stirring occasionally. Remove from heat; stir in the remaining 1 Tbsp. butter, the parsley, and chives.
4. Serve in shallow bowls with hot cooked rice.

PER SERVING (1 cup seafood mixture + ½ cup rice each) **CAL** 295, **FAT** 8 g (4 g sat. fat), **CHOL** 108 mg, **SODIUM** 490 mg, **CARB** 33 g (3 g fiber, 2 g sugars), **PRO** 21 g

White Beans and Tomatoes with Kale Pesto

35g CARB | SERVES 4
TOTAL 20 min.

- 2 tsp. olive oil
- 3 cups multicolor grape tomatoes, halved
- 2 15-oz. cans reduced-sodium cannellini beans, rinsed and drained
- ½ tsp. freshly ground black pepper
- 1 cup packed fresh baby kale
- ¼ cup finely shredded Parmesan cheese
- 2 Tbsp. pine nuts, toasted
- 1 Tbsp. water
- ½ tsp. lemon zest
- 1 Tbsp. lemon juice
- 1 clove garlic, peeled and halved
- ½ tsp. kosher salt

1. In a large nonstick skillet heat 1 tsp. of the oil over medium-high. Add tomatoes; cook about 2 minutes or until slightly soft, stirring occasionally. Add beans; cook about 3 minutes or until heated through, stirring occasionally. Stir in pepper.
2. Meanwhile, for pesto, combine the remaining ingredients in a food processor. Cover and process until nearly smooth, stopping to scrape down sides as necessary.
3. Top bean mixture with pesto.

PER SERVING (1 cup bean mixture + 2 Tbsp. pesto each) **CAL** 288, **FAT** 11 g (2 g sat. fat), **CHOL** 4 mg, **SODIUM** 435 mg, **CARB** 35 g (11 g fiber, 4 g sugars), **PRO** 14 g

Spanish
Shrimp and
Scallop
Sauté

**Black
Lentils with
Oranges
and Beets**

Slow Cooker
Vegetable Lasagna

**37g
CARB**

SERVES 8
HANDS ON 30 min.
SLOW COOK 5 hr.

- 1 cup chopped red bell pepper
- 4 oz. fresh cremini mushrooms (about 3 large), chopped
- 2 cups packed fresh baby spinach, coarsely chopped
- 1 24-oz. jar low-sodium red pasta sauce, any flavor
- 1 15-oz. can no-salt-added diced tomatoes, undrained
- 1 15-oz. carton part-skim ricotta cheese
- ¾ cup freshly grated Parmesan cheese
- 8 oz. oven-ready lasagna noodles (about 9 total)
- 2 cups shredded part-skim mozzarella cheese (8 oz.)
- ¼ cup chopped fresh basil

1. In a medium bowl combine bell pepper, mushrooms, and spinach. In a large bowl combine pasta sauce, tomatoes, ricotta, and ½ cup of the Parmesan.
2. Spread 1 cup of the sauce mixture in the bottom of a 6-qt. slow cooker. Place three noodles over sauce, breaking them as needed to fit in one layer. Spread another 1 cup sauce over the pasta. Layer with one-third of the vegetable mixture, three more noodles, and 1 cup sauce. Sprinkle with ½ cup of the mozzarella. Continue layering one-third of the vegetables, 1 cup sauce, ½ cup mozzarella, and the remaining noodles. Top with a final layer of the remaining vegetables, the remaining sauce, and the remaining 1 cup mozzarella.
3. Cover and cook on low 5 hours.
4. Turn off and unplug the slow cooker. Let lasagna stand, covered, 1 hour. Top servings with the remaining ¼ cup Parmesan and the basil.

PER SERVING *(1 cup each)* **CAL** 344,
FAT 12 g *(7 g sat. fat)*, **CHOL** 41 mg,
SODIUM 423 mg, **CARB** 37 g *(3 g fiber, 9 g sugars)*,
PRO 21 g,

Black Lentils with
Oranges and Beets

**44g
CARB**

SERVES 4
HANDS ON 25 min.
TOTAL 1 hr. 20 min.

- 1 8-oz. beet, greens removed
- ¾ cup dried black lentils
- ¾ tsp. kosher salt
- 2 Tbsp. pine nuts or chopped walnuts
- 1 orange
- 3 Tbsp. white balsamic vinegar
- 1 Tbsp. finely chopped shallot
- 1 Tbsp. olive oil
- 1 Tbsp. honey
- 1 tsp. chopped fresh rosemary
- ½ tsp. cracked black pepper
- 4 cups fresh arugula or baby kale
- 3 Tbsp. crumbled goat cheese (chèvre)

1. Preheat oven to 350°F. Trim beet, cutting off all but 1 inch of the stem and the roots. Wrap beet in foil and place on a small baking sheet. Bake about 1 hour 15 minutes or until tender; cool. Slip off and discard skin; slice beet.
2. Meanwhile, cook lentils according to package directions, adding ½ tsp. of the salt to cooking water; drain and cool. In a dry medium skillet toast pine nuts over medium 3 to 4 minutes or until golden and fragrant, stirring occasionally.
3. Remove zest from orange. Cut off white pith; cut orange into ¼-inch slices. For dressing, in a small bowl whisk together orange zest, the remaining ¼ tsp. salt, and the next six ingredients (through pepper).
4. In a large bowl toss together lentils and arugula. Arrange mixture on a platter. Top with beet and orange slices, cheese, and pine nuts; drizzle with dressing.

TIP Substitute a Chioggia beet for the red beet.

PER SERVING *(2 cups lentil mixture + about 1½ Tbsp. dressing each)* **CAL** 285,
FAT 8 g *(2 g sat. fat)*, **CHOL** 2 mg, **SODIUM** 287 mg,
CARB 44 g *(7 g fiber, 18 g sugars)*, **PRO** 12 g

Slow Cooker Vegetable Lasagna

QUICK TIP

To prevent condensation building up on the underside of the lid during the 1-hour rest time, place a paper towel under the lid.

Caponata
Sicilanata
with
Penne
Pasta

Farro with Roasted Sweet Potatoes and Watercress

42g
CARB

SERVES 4
HANDS ON 20 min.
TOTAL 45 min.

- ¾ cup pearled farro
- ¾ tsp. kosher salt
- 8 oz. sweet potato, peeled if desired and roughly chopped
- ½ cup sliced red onion
- 2 cloves garlic, minced
- 1 Tbsp. + 2 tsp. olive oil
- 1 tsp. smoked paprika
- 1 tsp. ground cumin
- 1 Tbsp. white balsamic vinegar
- 2 tsp. lemon juice
- 2 tsp. pure maple syrup
- 2 tsp. Dijon-style mustard
- 1 tsp. chopped fresh thyme
- ½ tsp. cracked black pepper
- 3 cups fresh watercress or arugula
- 2 Tbsp. chopped toasted walnuts

1. Preheat oven to 400°F. Cook farro according to package directions, adding ¼ tsp. of the salt to cooking water. Drain.
2. Line a 15×10-inch pan with parchment paper. In a large bowl combine sweet potatoes, onion, garlic, 1 Tbsp. of the oil, the smoked paprika, cumin, and ¼ tsp. of the salt (mixture will be dry). Spread sweet potato mixture, including any spices left in bowl, in a single layer on the prepared pan. Bake 20 to 25 minutes or until sweet potatoes are tender and onions and garlic are starting brown. Cool slightly.
3. For dressing, in a small bowl whisk together the remaining 2 tsp. oil and ¼ tsp. salt, the vinegar, lemon juice, maple syrup, mustard, thyme, and pepper.
4. Toss together farro, sweet potato mixture, watercress, walnuts, and dressing.

TO MAKE AHEAD Prepare as directed through Step 3. Transfer farro and sweet potatoes to an airtight container and the dressing to a separate container. Store in the refrigerator up to 3 days. To serve, toss farro, sweet potatoes, and dressing with greens and walnuts.

PER SERVING (1¼ cups each) **CAL** 271, **FAT** 9 g (1 g sat. fat), **CHOL** 0 mg, **SODIUM** 278 mg, **CARB** 42 g (6 g fiber, 6 g sugars), **PRO** 7 g

Caponata Sicilianata with Penne Pasta

57g
CARB

SERVES 4
HANDS ON 15 min.
SLOW COOK 3 hours 50 min.

- 1½ lb. eggplant, unpeeled and cut into ½-inch pieces
- 1 14.5-oz. can diced tomatoes with basil, garlic, and oregano, undrained
- 1½ cups thinly sliced celery
- 1 cup finely chopped red onion
- 1 cup ½-inch pieces red bell pepper
- ¼ to ⅓ cup golden raisins
- 2 Tbsp. balsamic vinegar
- ¼ to ½ tsp. crushed red pepper
- 2 cups water
- 1¼ cups no-boil, no-drain penne pasta
- ½ cup chopped fresh Italian parsley

- ¼ cup coarsely chopped pitted green olives
  Grated Parmesan cheese (optional)

1. In a 5- to 6-qt. slow cooker combine first eight ingredients (through crushed red pepper).
2. Cover and cook on low 3½ to 4½ hours or high 2 hours or until vegetables are nearly tender. If using low, turn to high. Stir in the water and pasta. Cover and cook about 20 minutes more or just until pasta is tender, stirring after 10 minutes.
3. Stir in parsley and olives. If desired, top individual servings with cheese.

TIP If you want a slightly sweeter sauce, stir in 1 to 2 tsp. honey.

PER SERVING (2½ cups each) **CAL** 267, **FAT** 3 g (0 g sat. fat), **CHOL** 0 mg, **SODIUM** 484 mg, **CARB** 57 g (10 g fiber, 22 g sugars), **PRO** 8 g

Farro with Roasted Sweet Potatoes and Watercress

QUICK TIP

For more fiber, leave the peel on the sweet potato.

5
SEASONAL
SIDES & SALADS

With a little creativity, you can turn a
ho-hum side dish into a good-for-you
temptation. Winter vegetables vie for
attention in this collection that gets a boost
from spices, simple sauces, and crispy
coatings. These easy sides and salads elevate
nutritious meal accompaniments from
humble to outstanding.

100

109

114

Fig and Walnut Wild Rice Dressing

Fig and Walnut Wild Rice Dressing

31g CARB

SERVES 8
HANDS ON 1 hr.
TOTAL 1 hr. 30 min.

Nonstick cooking spray
- 3 cups reduced-sodium chicken broth or vegetable broth
- ¾ cup wild rice
- ¾ cup brown rice
- 3 Tbsp. olive oil
- 2 cups finely chopped yellow onion
- 1 cup finely chopped celery
- ¼ tsp. ground nutmeg
- ¼ tsp. ground white or black pepper
- ¾ cup chopped fresh parsley
- ½ cup walnuts, chopped and toasted
- ¼ cup chopped dried Mission figs
- ¼ cup chopped fresh sage or 1½ tsp. dried sage, crushed

1. Preheat oven to 350°F. Coat a 2-qt. baking dish with cooking spray.
2. In a 3-qt. saucepan combine broth, wild rice, and brown rice. Bring to boiling; reduce heat. Cover and simmer 40 to 45 minutes or until rice is tender.
3. Meanwhile, in a large skillet heat oil over medium. Add onion, celery, nutmeg, and pepper; cook about 10 minutes or until tender. Transfer to a large bowl. Stir in the remaining ingredients.
4. Drain rice, reserving the cooking liquid. Add rice to the bowl. Measure 1 cup of the cooking liquid (if necessary, add additional broth or water to make 1 cup); stir into rice mixture. Transfer to the prepared baking dish; cover with foil.
5. Bake 25 minutes. Uncover; bake about 10 minutes more or until heated through.

PER SERVING (¾ cup each) **CAL** 240, **FAT** 11 g *(1 g sat. fat)*, **CHOL** 0 mg, **SODIUM** 40 mg, **CARB** 31 g *(3 g fiber, 4 g sugars)*, **PRO** 6 g

Creamed Corn with Red Peppers and Spinach

Creamed Corn with Red Peppers and Spinach

16g CARB

SERVES 10
HANDS ON 20 min.
SLOW COOK 3 hr.

- 4 cups fresh or frozen corn kernels, thawed if frozen
- 1½ cups chopped red bell peppers
- 1 cup chopped onion
- ¼ cup no-salt-added chicken broth
- 2 Tbsp. unsalted butter, melted
- ¼ tsp. salt
- ⅛ tsp. crushed red pepper
- 6 oz. fat-free cream cheese, cut into small chunks
- 4 cups fresh spinach, chopped
  Black pepper (optional)

1. In a 3½- or 4-qt. slow cooker combine the first seven ingredients (through crushed red pepper). Place cream cheese on top of the corn mixture. Cover and cook on low 3 hours or high 1½ hours.
2. Stir until mixture is well combined. Gently stir in spinach. Serve immediately. If desired, sprinkle with pepper.

PER SERVING (½ cup each) **CAL** 108, **FAT** 3 g *(2 g sat. fat)*, **CHOL** 8 mg, **SODIUM** 202 mg, **CARB** 16 g *(2 g fiber, 7 g sugars)*, **PRO** 6 g

Mashed Root Vegetables with Parmesan

8g CARB

SERVES 8
HANDS ON 25 min.
TOTAL 1 hr. 2 min.

- 3 lb. assorted root vegetables, such as carrots, parsnips, turnips, rutabaga, and/or red or yellow potatoes
- 3 cloves garlic, peeled
- ½ tsp. salt
- ¼ cup fat-free milk
- 1 Tbsp. olive oil
- 1 Tbsp. butter
- ¼ to ½ tsp. black pepper
- ¼ cup chopped fresh Italian parsley
- ½ cup shredded Parmesan cheese (2 oz.)

1. Preheat oven to 400°F. Peel root vegetables; cut vegetables into 2- to 3-inch pieces. In a 4-qt. saucepan combine vegetables, garlic, and ¼ tsp. of the salt; add enough cold water to cover. Bring to boiling; reduce heat. Cover and simmer about 20 minutes or until very tender. Meanwhile, in a 1-qt. saucepan heat milk, olive oil, and butter over low until butter melts.
2. Drain vegetables; return to pan. Mash vegetables. Stir milk mixture, the remaining salt, and pepper to taste into vegetables. Stir in half of the parsley and half of the Parmesan. Spread mashed vegetable mixture in a 1½-qt. gratin dish. Top with the remaining cheese.
3. Bake, uncovered, about 15 minutes or until cheese is melted and vegetables are heated through. If desired, preheat broiler; broil vegetables 4 to 5 inches from the heat about 2 minutes or until top is browned. Top with the remaining parsley.

TO MAKE AHEAD Prepare as directed through Step 2, except cool mashed vegetable mixture slightly before topping with Parmesan cheese. Cover and chill up to 24 hours. Uncover; bake in a preheated 400°F oven about 30 minutes or until heated through. Continue as directed.

PER SERVING (⅔ cup each) **CAL** 81, **FAT** 5 g (2 g sat. fat), **CHOL** 8 mg, **SODIUM** 260 mg, **CARB** 8 g (1 g fiber, 2 g sugars), **PRO** 3 g

Herb-Roasted Root Vegetables

Herb-Roasted Root Vegetables

27g CARB

SERVES 8
HANDS ON 45 min.
TOTAL 1 hr. 15 min.

- Nonstick cooking spray
- 3 Tbsp. olive oil
- 2 Tbsp. honey
- 2 Tbsp. minced fresh garlic
- 2 Tbsp. chopped fresh thyme
- 2 Tbsp. chopped fresh rosemary
- ½ tsp. salt
- ½ tsp. black pepper
- 1½ lb. butternut squash, peeled, seeded, and cut into ½-inch cubes
- 1 lb. celery root, peeled and cut into ½-inch cubes
- 1 lb. Brussels sprouts, trimmed and halved
- 4 shallots, cut into wedges
- 1 lemon, quartered

1. Set racks in the upper and lower thirds of oven; preheat oven to 425°F. Coat two 15×10-inch baking pans with cooking spray.
2. In a large bowl whisk together the next seven ingredients (through pepper). Add squash, celery root, Brussels sprouts, shallots, and lemon; toss to coat. Divide vegetables between the prepared pans, spreading evenly.
3. Roast 45 to 60 minutes or until tender and charred, rotating pans and stirring vegetables halfway through cooking. Cool slightly, then squeeze roasted lemons over the vegetables.

TIP To save on prep, look for cubed butternut squash in the produce section of your supermarket.

PER SERVING (1 cup each) **CAL** 156, **FAT** 6 g (1 g sat. fat), **CHOL** 0 mg, **SODIUM** 294 mg, **CARB** 27 g (6 g fiber, 8 g sugars), **PRO** 4 g

Mashed Root Vegetables with Parmesan

Sweet and Spiced Roasted Carrots

19g CARB

SERVES 4
HANDS ON 10 min.
TOTAL 50 min.

- 8 medium carrots, cut into 2-inch pieces (4 cups)
- 2 Tbsp. packed brown sugar
- 5 tsp. butter, melted
- ¼ tsp. ground cinnamon
- ⅛ tsp. salt
- ⅛ tsp. ground cloves (optional)
  Dash cayenne pepper
- 2 Tbsp. chopped, toasted pecans

1. Preheat oven to 425°F. Line a 13×9-inch baking pan with parchment paper. Arrange carrots in an even layer in the prepared pan. Cover with foil. Roast 30 minutes.
2. Meanwhile, in a small bowl stir together next 6 ingredients (through cayenne) until well combined. Spoon sugar mixture over carrots; stir to coat.
3. Roast, uncovered, about 10 minutes more or until carrots are tender and glazed. Sprinkle with pecans.

PER SERVING (⅔ cup each) **CAL** 143. **FAT** 8 g (3 g sat. fat), **CHOL** 13 mg, **SODIUM** 197 mg, **CARB** 19 g (4 g fiber, 13 g sugars), **PRO** 2 g

QUICK TIP

If you can find slender baby carrots, use them whole in place of cut carrots.

Caraway Whole-Roasted Cauliflower

12g
CARB

SERVES 4
HANDS ON 30 min.
TOTAL 1 hr. 15 min.

- 2 Tbsp. olive oil
- 1 Tbsp. stone-ground mustard
- 2 tsp. caraway seeds, toasted and crushed
- 1 tsp. kosher salt
- 1 2- to 2½-lb. head cauliflower, trimmed
- ¼ cup water
- ½ cup sliced red onion
- ⅓ cup red wine vinegar
- 1 tsp. sugar
- ½ tsp. kosher salt
- ¼ cup snipped dried apricots

1. Preheat oven to 425°F. In a small bowl whisk together olive oil, mustard, caraway seeds, and salt. Spread caraway mixture over the cauliflower. Place water in a large cast-iron or other ovenproof skillet. Place cauliflower in skillet; cover with foil. Bake 30 minutes.

2. Meanwhile, for pickled onion, in a small bowl combine the onion, vinegar, sugar, and salt; set aside, stirring occasionally.

3. Uncover cauliflower and increase oven temperature to 450°F. Continue roasting, uncovered, about 30 minutes more or until golden brown and tender. Serve with pickled onion, dried apricots, and, if desired, additional mustard.

PER SERVING (¼ head cauliflower each) **CAL** 115, **FAT** 7 g (1 g sat. fat), **CHOL** 0 mg, **SODIUM** 390 mg, **CARB** 12 g (3 g fiber, 7 g sugars), **PRO** 2 g

Sour Cream-Chive Mashed Carrots and Parsnips

Brined Skillet-Roasted Brussels Sprouts

9g
CARB

SERVES 6
HANDS ON 20 min.
TOTAL 1 hr. 45 min.

1½ **lb. Brussels sprouts**
8 **cups cold water**
½ **cup kosher salt**
¼ **cup olive oil**
1 **tsp. mustard seeds**
¼ **tsp. cracked black pepper**
¼ **tsp. kosher salt (optional)**

1. Trim stems and remove any wilted outer leaves from Brussels sprouts. Halve any large sprouts. For brine, in an extra-large bowl or deep container combine the cold water and the ½ cup salt, stirring until salt is completely dissolved. Add Brussels sprouts, making sure sprouts are completely submerged (if necessary, weight sprouts down with a plate). Let stand at room temperature 1 hour.
2. Preheat oven to 350°F. Drain Brussels sprouts; do not rinse. Transfer sprouts to an extra-large cast-iron skillet or shallow roasting pan. Drizzle with oil; toss to coat. Roast 25 to 30 minutes or until tender, stirring once.
3. Meanwhile, in a small skillet heat mustard seeds over medium-low about 5 minutes or until lightly toasted, shaking skillet occasionally. Remove seeds from skillet; crush slightly. Sprinkle crushed seeds, pepper, and, if desired, the ¼ tsp. salt over cooked Brussels sprouts; toss gently to combine.

PER SERVING (½ cup each) **CAL** 126, **FAT** 9 g (1 g sat. fat), **CHOL** 0 mg, **SODIUM** 346 mg, **CARB** 9 g (4 g fiber, 2 g sugars), **PRO** 4 g

Sour Cream-Chive Mashed Carrots and Parsnips

17g
CARB

SERVES 6
HANDS ON 20 min.
TOTAL 45 min.

4 **cups 1-inch pieces carrots (8 medium)**
2 **cups 1-inch pieces peeled parsnips (2 to 3 medium)**
⅓ **cup light sour cream**
3 **Tbsp. chopped fresh chives**
2 **Tbsp. fat-free milk**
2 **Tbsp. butter**
¼ **tsp. salt**
⅛ **tsp. black pepper**

1. In a 4-qt. saucepan cook vegetables, covered, in enough boiling lightly salted water to cover 25 to 30 minutes or until vegetables are very tender. Drain well; return to saucepan.
2. Use a potato masher or ricer to finely mash carrots and parsnips. Add sour cream, 2 Tbsp. of the chives, the milk, butter, salt, and pepper. Cook and stir over medium-low until heated through.
3. Transfer mashed vegetables to a serving bowl. Sprinkle with the remaining chives.

PER SERVING (½ cup each) **CAL** 117, **FAT** 5 g (3 g sat. fat), **CHOL** 14 mg, **SODIUM** 199 mg, **CARB** 17 g (4 g fiber, 6 g sugars), **PRO** 2 g

Brined
Skillet-Roasted
Brussels
Sprouts

Honey and
Ginger
Roasted
Turnips

Honey and Ginger Roasted Turnips

22g CARB

SERVES 4
HANDS ON 15 min.
TOTAL 45 min.

- 2 lb. turnips, peeled and cut into 1-inch cubes
- 1 Tbsp. olive oil
- 3 cloves garlic, minced
- 1 Tbsp. grated fresh ginger
- 1 Tbsp. chopped fresh thyme or 1 tsp. dried thyme, crushed
- 2 Tbsp. honey
- 1 Tbsp. white wine vinegar
- ⅛ tsp. ground nutmeg
  Black pepper to taste
- 3 strips thick-sliced bacon, chopped, crisp-cooked, and drained

1. Position a rack in lower middle of oven; preheat oven to 425°F.

2. In a large bowl combine turnips, oil, garlic, ginger, and 2 tsp. of the fresh thyme (or ½ tsp. of the dried thyme); toss to coat. Spread in a single layer on a baking sheet. Roast 30 to 35 minutes or until tender and golden, turning once.

3. In a large bowl whisk together honey, vinegar, and nutmeg. Add roasted turnips; toss to coat and season with pepper. Stir in bacon and the remaining 1 tsp. fresh thyme (or ½ tsp. dried thyme).

PER SERVING *(1 cup each)* **CAL** 158, **FAT** 7 g *(2 g sat. fat)*, **CHOL** 6 mg, **SODIUM** 244 mg, **CARB** 22 g *(3 g fiber, 16 g sugars)*, **PRO** 4 g

Roasted Broccoli with Garlicky Tahini Sauce

Roasted Broccoli with Garlicky Tahini Sauce

8g CARB

SERVES 8
TOTAL 25 min.

- 1½ lb. broccoli
- 1 Tbsp. olive oil
- ½ tsp. black pepper
- 2 Tbsp. tahini
- 2 Tbsp. lemon juice
- 1 Tbsp. honey
- 1 Tbsp. reduced-sodium soy sauce
- 2 cloves garlic, minced
- ½ tsp. ground coriander
- ⅓ cup thinly sliced green onions
- ⅓ cup coarsely chopped cilantro
- 1 tsp. toasted sesame seeds

1. Position a rack in bottom third of oven; set a 15×10-inch baking pan on the rack. Preheat oven to 500°F.

2. Cut broccoli florets into 1-inch pieces. Peel tough outer layer from the broccoli stalks. Cut peeled stalks into 2-inch-long pieces, then slice into ½-inch-thick planks. In a large bowl toss broccoli with oil and pepper to coat.

3. Spread the broccoli in an even layer in the hot pan. Roast 9 to 10 minutes or until tender and starting to brown.

4. In a large bowl whisk the next six ingredients (through coriander). Add the broccoli, green onions, and cilantro; toss to coat. Sprinkle with sesame seeds.

PER SERVING *(⅔ cups each)* **CAL** 70, **FAT** 4 g *(1 g sat. fat)*, **CHOL** 0 mg, **SODIUM** 74 mg, **CARB** 8 g *(2 g fiber, 3 g sugars)*, **PRO** 3 g

Cumin-Scented Peas
with Cilantro

10g
CARB

SERVES 6
TOTAL 10 min.

- **2** tsp. vegetable oil
- **1** tsp. cumin seeds, crushed
- **¼** to ½ tsp. crushed red pepper (optional)
- **1** 16-oz. pkg. frozen peas, thawed
- **2** Tbsp. chopped fresh cilantro
  Salt (optional)

1. In a large saucepan heat oil over medium-high. Add cumin and crushed red pepper (if using); cook and stir 30 seconds or until fragrant. Stir in peas. Cook 3 minutes, stirring occasionally. Add cilantro; cook and stir 30 seconds more. If desired, season to taste with salt.

PER SERVING (½ cup each) **CAL** 73, **FAT** 2 g (0 g sat. fat), **CHOL** 0 mg, **SODIUM** 82 mg, **CARB** 10 g (3 g fiber, 4 g sugars), **PRO** 4 g,

Crispy Parmesan Roasted Butternut Squash

18g CARB | SERVES 4
HANDS ON 20 min.
TOTAL 45 min.

Nonstick cooking spray
1 1½- to 1¾-lb. butternut squash, peeled, seeded, and cut into ¾-inch pieces
2 Tbsp. olive oil
½ tsp. kosher salt
⅛ tsp. black pepper
⅓ cup grated Parmesan cheese
¼ tsp. dried thyme, sage, or basil, crushed

1. Preheat oven to 450°F. Coat a 15×10-inch baking pan with cooking spray. Place squash in prepared pan. Drizzle with oil and sprinkle with salt and pepper; toss to coat.
2. Roast 15 minutes. Stir squash; roast 5 minutes more. Stir in cheese and thyme. Roast about 5 minutes more or until squash is tender.

PER SERVING (½ cup each) **CAL** 154, **FAT** 9 g (2 g sat. fat), **CHOL** 6 mg, **SODIUM** 267 mg, **CARB** 18 g (3 g fiber, 3 g sugars), **PRO** 3 g

QUICK TIP
To save time, use packaged precut fresh butternut squash.

Bacon-Roasted Sweet Potatoes and Shallots with Blistered Grapes

Bacon-Roasted Sweet Potatoes and Shallots with Blistered Grapes

39g CARB | **SERVES** 8
HANDS ON 25 min.
TOTAL 55 min.

- 6 oz. reduced-sodium, less-fat bacon, coarsely chopped
- 2¼ lb. sweet potatoes, cut into 2-inch pieces
- 10 oz. shallots, peeled and halved or quartered
- 3 Tbsp. canola oil
- ½ tsp. kosher salt
- ½ tsp. pepper
- 2 cups red or green seedless grapes

1. Preheat oven to 450°F. In a large skillet cook bacon until crisp; drain bacon on paper towels. Place a 15×10-inch baking pan in the oven 5 minutes.
2. In a large bowl toss together the sweet potatoes, shallots, canola oil, salt, and pepper. Transfer sweet potato mixture to hot baking pan.
3. Roast 30 minutes or until tender, stirring once and adding grapes to the pan the last 5 minutes of roasting. Top cooked potato and grape mixture with reserved bacon.

PER SERVING (¾ cup each) **CAL** 224,
FAT 6 g (1 g sat. fat), **CHOL** 3 mg, **SODIUM** 198 mg,
CARB 39 g (5 g fiber, 14 g sugars), **PRO** 5 g

Smoky Mashed Sweet Potatoes

Smoky Mashed Sweet Potatoes

48g CARB | **SERVES** 8
HANDS ON 45 min.
TOTAL 1 hr.

- 4 lb. sweet potatoes, peeled and cut into ½-inch pieces
- ¾ cup fat-free milk
- 5 Tbsp. unsalted butter
- 5 cloves garlic, coarsely chopped
- 4 sprigs fresh thyme
- 1½ tsp. smoked paprika
- 2 tsp. chopped fresh thyme
- 1 tsp. salt
- ½ tsp. grated orange zest
- ⅛ tsp. cayenne pepper
- ¼ cup chopped green onions

1. In a large pot combine sweet potatoes, milk, butter, garlic, and thyme sprigs. Cover and cook over low 30 to 45 minute or until potatoes are tender, stirring occasionally
2. Cool slightly. Discard thyme sprigs. Transfer sweet potato mixture to a food processor. Add paprika, chopped thyme, salt, orange zest, and cayenne. Cover and process until smooth. Stir in green onions.

PER SERVING (¾ cup each) **CAL** 272,
FAT 7 g (5 g sat. fat), **CHOL** 20 mg,
SODIUM 427 mg, **CARB** 48 g (7 g fiber,
11 g sugars), **PRO** 5 g

Pickled Sweet Potatoes

Brussels Sprouts Salad with Hazelnuts

6g
CARB | **SERVES** 8
TOTAL 25 min.

- 1   lb. Brussels sprouts
- 2   Tbsp. water
- ½   cup hazelnuts, toasted and coarsely chopped
- ½   cup finely shredded Pecorino Romano cheese (2 oz.)
- ¼   cup red wine vinegar
- 3   Tbsp. olive oil
- ¼   tsp. salt
- ¼   tsp. black pepper
      Shaved Pecorino Romano cheese (optional)

1. Trim stems and remove any wilted outer leaves from Brussels sprouts. Thinly slice sprouts. In a microwave-safe dish combine Brussels sprouts and the water; cover with vented plastic wrap. Microwave about 3 minutes or until sprouts are bright green, stirring once. Drain in a colander. Rinse with cold water to cool; drain again. Pat dry with paper towels or use a salad spinner to dry.

2. In a large bowl combine Brussels sprouts, hazelnuts, and the ½ cup shredded cheese. For dressing, in a small screw-top jar combine vinegar, oil, salt, and pepper. Cover and shake well to combine. Pour dressing over sprouts mixture; toss gently to coat. If desired, top with shaved cheese.

TIP To thinly slice Brussels sprouts, use the thin slicing blade of a food processor. Or halve the sprouts lengthwise with a sharp knife, then place halves, cut sides down, on a cutting board and cut into thin slices.

PER SERVING (⅔ cup each) **CAL** 141, **FAT** 12 g (2 g sat. fat), **CHOL** 5 mg, **SODIUM** 146 mg, **CARB** 6 g (3 g fiber, 2 g sugars), **PRO** 5 g

Pickled Sweet Potatoes

25g
CARB | **SERVES** 8
HANDS ON 25 min.
TOTAL 1 hr. 25 min.

- 1¼   cups rice vinegar
- 1¼   cups water
- ¼   cup sugar
- 1   Tbsp. salt
- 2   chopped and seeded Anaheim chile peppers (tip, *p. 154*)
- 1   cup thinly sliced red onion
- 2   large peeled sweet potatoes

1. In a 4-qt. nonreactive saucepan combine vinegar, water, sugar, and salt. In a large heatproof bowl combine chiles and red onion. Using a mandoline, slice potatoes about ¹⁄₁₆ inch thick; add to vinegar mixture. Bring to boiling; reduce heat. Simmer, uncovered, 2 minutes. Pour potatoes and vinegar mixture over onion mixture. Let stand 1 hour before serving or cover and refrigerate up to 1 week.

PER SERVING (about ⅔ cup each) **CAL** 109, **FAT** 0 g, **CHOL** 0 mg, **SODIUM** 180 mg, **CARB** 25 g (3 g fiber, 6 g sugars), **PRO** 2 g

Brussels
Sprouts
Salad with
Hazelnuts

Kale,
Cranberry,
and Root
Vegetable
Salad

Kale, Cranberry, and Root Vegetable Salad

20g CARB

SERVES 10
HANDS ON 30 min.
TOTAL 2 hr.

- 3 medium beets, trimmed, peeled, quartered, and sliced ¼ inch thick
- 5 medium carrots, sliced ¼ inch thick
- 3 Tbsp. olive oil
- ½ tsp. sea salt
- ½ tsp. cracked black pepper
- 4 medium shallots, peeled and quartered lengthwise
- ¾ cup fresh or frozen cranberries, coarsely chopped
- 1 8-oz. bunch kale, stems removed and leaves cut into ½-inch-thick ribbons (6 cups)
- ⅓ cup golden raisins
- 2 Tbsp. lemon juice
- 1 Tbsp. honey mustard
- 2 cloves garlic, minced
- 1 tsp. grated fresh ginger
- ¼ cup chopped toasted pecans, roasted and salted sunflower seeds, or roasted and salted pumpkin seeds (pepitas)

1. Place a 15×10-inch baking pan in oven; preheat oven to 425°F. Meanwhile, in an extra-large bowl combine beets, carrots, 2 Tbsp. of the oil, the salt, and pepper; toss to coat. Carefully spread carrots and beets in hot pan in an even layer. Roast 10 minutes. Add shallots and cranberries to pan, stirring to coat. Roast 20 to 25 minutes more or until vegetables are just tender, stirring once.

2. Place kale in the extra-large bowl. Add the remaining 1 Tbsp. oil. Using your fingers, massage kale until bright green and tender. In a small bowl combine raisins, lemon juice, mustard, garlic, and ginger.

3. Add raisin mixture to roasted vegetables; stir to coat. Cool 5 minutes. Add vegetable-raisin mixture to kale; toss to combine. Let stand at least 30 minutes. Serve at room temperature. Or cover and refrigerate up to 4 hours; bring to room temperature and stir before serving. Sprinkle with pecans.

PER SERVING (1 cup each) **CAL** 154, **FAT** 7 g (1 g sat. fat), **CHOL** 0 mg, **SODIUM** 156 mg, **CARB** 20 g (5 g fiber, 10 g sugars), **PRO** 5 g

Green Bean Casserole Salad

Green Bean Casserole Salad

14g CARB

SERVES 8
HANDS ON 25 min.
TOTAL 35 min.

- 3 Tbsp. olive oil
- ½ cup thinly sliced shallots
- 3 cups cubed sourdough bread
- 3 cups sliced fresh cremini mushrooms
- 1 lb. fresh green beans, trimmed and halved
- ¼ cup water
- 1 Tbsp. Dijon-style mustard
- 1 Tbsp. white wine vinegar
- 3 cloves garlic, minced
- 1 Tbsp. fresh thyme or 1 tsp. dried thyme, crushed
- ½ tsp. salt
  Black pepper to taste
- 1 bunch chard, leaves coarsely chopped (about 4 cups)

1. In a large skillet heat 2 Tbsp. of the oil over medium-high until very hot but not smoking. Add half of the shallots; cook and stir 3 to 4 minutes or until golden brown and crisp. Using a slotted spoon, transfer fried shallots to a paper towel-lined plate. Repeat with the remaining shallots. Leave any remaining oil in the pan. Reduce heat to medium.

2. Add bread cubes to pan; cook 5 to 6 minutes or until toasted, turning occasionally. Transfer croutons to a bowl.

3. Add the remaining 1 Tbsp. oil to the pan; heat over medium-high. Add mushrooms; cook about 6 minutes or until golden brown, stirring occasionally. Transfer to a bowl.

4. Add green beans and the water to the pan; cover and cook over medium 5 to 6 minutes or until tender.

5. Meanwhile, in a small bowl whisk together mustard, vinegar, garlic, thyme, salt, and pepper. Add to beans; cook 30 seconds more. Remove pan from heat. Stir in chard, mushrooms, and croutons. Top with the reserved shallots.

PER SERVING (1 cup each) **CAL** 116, **FAT** 6 g (1 g sat. fat), **CHOL** 0 mg, **SODIUM** 299 mg, **CARB** 14 g (2 g fiber, 3 g sugars), **PRO** 4 g

Fennel and Grapefruit Salad

Roasted Squash Spinach Salad

34g CARB

SERVES 4	
HANDS ON 25 min.	
TOTAL 50 min.	

- 1   1-lb. butternut squash
- 2   Tbsp. olive oil
- ¼   tsp. salt
- ⅔   cup balsamic vinegar
- 1   tsp. honey
- 8   cups fresh baby spinach
- ½   cup very thinly sliced red onion
- ½   cup finely shredded Parmesan cheese (2 oz.)
- ⅓   cup dried cranberries
- ¼   cup sliced almonds, toasted

1. Preheat oven to 425°F. Line a 15×10-inch baking pan with foil. Cut squash in half lengthwise; remove and reserve seeds. Peel squash and trim ends. Cut squash into ½-inch slices; place in the prepared pan. Brush with 1 Tbsp. of the oil and sprinkle with ⅛ tsp. of the salt. Roast 20 minutes.
2. Meanwhile, remove and discard large pieces of squash strings from seeds. In a medium bowl combine seeds and enough cold water to cover. Using your fingers, separate strings from seeds; discard strings. Rinse and drain seeds; pat dry on paper towels. In a small bowl toss seeds with the remaining 1 Tbsp. oil and ⅛ tsp. salt.
3. Sprinkle squash with seeds. Roast about 5 minutes more or just until squash is tender. Cool slightly.
4. For balsamic drizzle, in a 1-qt. saucepan bring vinegar to boiling; reduce heat. Boil gently, uncovered, 5 to 8 minutes or until reduced to ¼ cup (it will reduce quickly at the end, so watch carefully). Remove from heat; whisk in honey. Cool slightly.
5. In a salad bowl combine spinach, red onion, and squash slices. Spoon balsamic drizzle over spinach mixture and sprinkle with cheese, cranberries, almonds, and squash seeds.

PER SERVING *(2½ cups each)* **CAL** 272, **FAT** 13 g *(3 g sat. fat)*, **CHOL** 7 mg, **SODIUM** 373 mg, **CARB** 34 g *(5 g fiber, 18 g sugars)*, **PRO** 8 g

Fennel and Grapefruit Salad

19g CARB

SERVES 4	
TOTAL 15 min.	

- 1   large grapefruit
- 1   tsp. honey
- 1   tsp. Dijon-style mustard
- ¼   tsp. salt
- ⅛   tsp. black pepper
- 1   Tbsp. + 1 tsp. canola oil
- 1   small fennel bulb, cored and thinly sliced (if desired, reserve fennel fronds for garnish)
- 1   medium Granny Smith apple, cored and thinly sliced
- 1   Tbsp. toasted sunflower seeds

1. Remove 1 Tbsp. zest from grapefruit. Place in a large bowl.
2. Cut a thin slice from both ends of grapefruit. Place a flat end on a cutting board and cut away the peel and white part of the rind. Holding the grapefruit over the bowl with zest to catch juices, cut into center between one side of segment and membrane. Cut along other side of segment next to membrane to free segment. Repeat to remove all segments. Cut segments into thirds and place in another bowl.
3. For dressing, squeeze the membranes into bowl with zest to get 2 Tbsp. juice total. Add honey, mustard, salt, and pepper; whisk to combine. Whisk in the oil.
4. Add fennel, apple, and grapefruit segments to dressing; toss to combine. Sprinkle with sunflower seeds. If desired, garnish with fennel fronds.

PER SERVING *(1 cup each)* **CAL** 130, **FAT** 6 g *(1 g sat. fat)*, **CHOL** 0 mg, **SODIUM** 206 mg, **CARB** 19 g *(4 g fiber, 14 g sugars)*, **PRO** 2 g

QUICK TIP

For attractive
half-rings, look for a
squash that is long
and narrow.

**Roasted
Squash
Spinach
Salad**

6

FRESH-BAKED
BREADS

The holidays wouldn't be complete without
bread. From muffins to dinner rolls, these
slimmed-down versions get their goodness
using whole grains, nutritious stir-ins, and
healthful portion sizes. Check out trendy
no-knead bread, fruit-filled muffins,
savory scones, and seeded breadsticks, plus
options with popular pumpkin.

**Rosemary-Parmesan
Bread with Garlic Butter**

Caption: Rosemary-Parmesan Bread with Garlic Butter

Two-Tone Balsamic-Onion Spiral Rolls

29g
CARB

SERVES servings
HANDS ON 35 min.
TOTAL 2 hr.

- 2 slices bacon
- 2 cups chopped onions
- ¼ cup balsamic vinegar
- ½ cup grated Parmesan cheese
- ¼ tsp. black pepper
- 1 1-lb. loaf frozen white bread dough, thawed
- 1 1-lb. loaf frozen whole wheat bread dough, thawed
- 1 egg yolk, lightly beaten
- 1 Tbsp. milk

1. Grease a 13×9-inch baking pan. In a large skillet cook bacon until crisp. Using a slotted spoon, transfer bacon to paper towels, reserving drippings in skillet. Crumble bacon. Add onions to skillet; cook over medium about 5 minutes or until tender. Carefully stir in balsamic vinegar. Simmer, uncovered, over medium-low 1 to 2 minutes or until most of the liquid has evaporated. Remove from heat. Stir in Parmesan cheese and pepper. Cool completely.
2. Meanwhile, on a lightly floured surface roll each loaf of bread dough into a 16×10-inch rectangle. Spread onion mixture over white dough rectangle; sprinkle with bacon. Top with wheat dough rectangle. Starting from a long side, roll up rectangles together. Pinch seam to seal. Slice roll crosswise into 16 pieces. Place pieces, cut sides down, in the prepared pan.
3. Cover loosely and let rise in a warm place until nearly double in size (about 45 minutes). Meanwhile, preheat oven to 375°F. In a small bowl beat together egg yolk and milk; brush over rolls.
4. Bake, uncovered, about 25 minutes or until roll tops are light brown. Invert rolls onto a wire rack. Remove pan. Cool slightly. Invert again onto a platter. Serve warm.

PER SERVING (1 roll each) **CAL** 189,
FAT 4 g (1 g sat. fat), **CHOL** 18 mg, **SODIUM** 237 mg,
CARB 29 g (1 g fiber, 2 g sugars), **PRO** 7 g

Rosemary-Parmesan Bread with Garlic Butter

18g
CARB

SERVES 16
HANDS ON 25 min.
TOTAL 4 hr. 30 min.

- 1½ cups warm water (105°F to 115°F)
- 1 pkg. active dry yeast
- 2⅔ cups all-purpose flour
- ⅓ cup finely shredded Parmesan cheese
- 3 Tbsp. whole wheat flour
- 1 Tbsp. finely chopped fresh rosemary
- 1½ tsp. salt
  Nonstick cooking spray
- 1 Tbsp. yellow cornmeal
- 2 Tbsp. butter, melted
- ¼ tsp. garlic salt

1. In an extra-large bowl stir together the warm water and yeast; let stand 5 minutes. Add the next five ingredients (through salt) to yeast mixture; stir just until combined. Stir with a wooden spoon about 1 minute more or until mixture forms a ball. (Dough will be very soft and sticky.)

Cover bowl with plastic wrap; let stand at room temperature 2 hours.
2. Lightly coat a 5- to 6-qt. slow cooker with cooking spray. Line the bottom of the cooker with parchment paper; coat paper with cooking spray and sprinkle with cornmeal. Turn dough out onto a well-floured surface; shape dough into a ball. Place in the center of the prepared cooker.
3. Cover and cook on high about 2 hours or until temperature in center of loaf registers 200°F, giving the crockery liner a half-turn halfway through cooking if possible. (Do not lift the lid.)
4. Preheat broiler. Remove bread from cooker; peel off parchment paper. Place bread on an ungreased baking sheet. Broil 4 to 6 inches from the heat 3 to 4 minutes or until bread is golden and surface is no longer moist. Transfer to a wire rack. Brush with melted butter; sprinkle with garlic salt. Cool completely before slicing.

PER SERVING (1 slice each) **CAL** 104,
FAT 2 g (1 g sat. fat), **CHOL** 5 mg, **SODIUM** 283 mg,
CARB 18 g (1 g fiber, 0 g sugars), **PRO** 3 g

QUICK TIP

This recipe is easily doubled. Use two 13×9-inch pans and double all ingredients.

Two-Tone Balsamic-Onion Spiral Rolls

Tomato-Bacon Breadsticks

Potato Bread

20g
CARB

SERVES 24
HANDS ON 55 min.
TOTAL 3 hr. 25 min.

2 cups water
1¾ cups cubed, peeled russet or long white potato
¼ cup butter, cut up
1½ tsp. salt
4½ to 4¾ cups all-purpose flour
2 pkg. active dry yeast
2 eggs

1. In a medium saucepan bring the water and potato to boiling; reduce heat. Simmer, covered, 12 to 15 minutes or until very tender. Drain, reserving 1 cup of the hot cooking water. Mash potato (should have 1 cup).
2. In a small bowl combine reserved 1 cup cooking water, the butter, and salt. Cool to 120°F to 130°F.
3. In a large bowl stir together 2 cups of the flour and the yeast. Add butter mixture and eggs. Beat with a mixer on low 30 seconds, scraping bowl constantly. Beat on high 3 minutes. Stir in mashed potato and as much of the remaining flour as you can.
4. Turn dough out onto a lightly floured surface. Knead in enough of the remaining flour to make a moderately stiff dough that is smooth and elastic (6 to 8 minutes total). Shape dough into a ball. Place in a lightly greased bowl, turning to grease surface of dough. Cover and let rise in a warm place until double in size (1 to 1½ hours).
5. Punch dough down. Turn out onto a lightly floured surface; divide in half. Cover and let rest 10 minutes. Meanwhile, lightly grease two 8×4-inch loaf pans.
6. Shape each dough half into a loaf by patting or rolling. Place shaped dough halves, seam sides down, in prepared loaf pans. Lightly sprinkle tops with additional flour. Cover and let rise in a warm place until nearly double in size (30 to 40 minutes).
7. Preheat oven to 375°F. Bake 35 to 40 minutes or until bread sounds hollow when lightly tapped (if necessary to prevent overbrowning, cover loosely with foil the last 15 minutes). Immediately remove bread from pans; cool on wire racks.

PER SERVING (1 slice each) **CAL** 119,
FAT 3 g (1 g sat. fat), **CHOL** 23 mg, **SODIUM** 167 mg,
CARB 20 g (1 g fiber, 0 g sugars), **PRO** 3 g

Tomato-Bacon Breadsticks

9g
CARB

SERVES 16
HANDS ON 25 min.
TOTAL 35 min.

4 slices turkey bacon
¼ cup dried tomatoes (not oil pack) Boiling water
1 cup all-purpose flour
½ cup whole wheat pastry flour or whole wheat flour
2 tsp. baking powder
½ tsp. salt
¼ tsp. cream of tartar
2 Tbsp. chopped green onion tops
⅓ cup 60% to 70% vegetable oil spread, chilled
1 Tbsp. butter
½ cup fat-free milk Nonstick cooking spray
¼ cup grated Parmesan cheese (1 oz.)

1. Preheat oven to 425°F. Cook bacon according to package directions; cool slightly and crumble or chop bacon. Place tomatoes in a small bowl. Add enough boiling water to cover; let stand 5 minutes. Drain tomatoes, discarding liquid. Finely chop tomatoes.
2. In a medium bowl stir together the next five ingredients (through cream of tartar). Stir in green onion tops. Using a pastry blender, cut in vegetable oil spread and butter until mixture resembles coarse crumbs. Stir in crumbled bacon and chopped tomatoes. Make a well in the center of the flour mixture. Add milk; stir just until dough clings together.
3. Turn dough out onto a lightly floured surface. Knead by folding and gently pressing dough four to six strokes or until nearly smooth. Roll dough into an 8-inch square. Cut into 1-inch-wide strips; cut each strip in half crosswise. If desired, twist each strip.
4. Place strips 1 inch apart on an ungreased baking sheet. Coat with cooking spray; sprinkle with Parmesan cheese. Bake 8 to 10 minutes or until tops are golden brown. Serve warm.

PER SERVING (1 breadstick each) **CAL** 94,
FAT 5 g (2 g sat. fat), **CHOL** 6 mg, **SODIUM** 251 mg,
CARB 9 g (1 g fiber, 1 g sugars), **PRO** 3 g

POTATO ROLLS

Prepare as directed through Step 5, except grease two large baking sheets. Divide each dough half into 12 pieces. Shape into balls; lightly dip tops in additional flour. Arrange balls 1½ inches apart on the prepared baking sheets. Bake 20 to 25 minutes or until golden. Remove from baking sheets; cool on wire racks.

Cracked Black Pepper and Rosemary Focaccia

let rise in a warm place 30 minutes.
5. Preheat oven to 375°F. Bake about 25 minutes or until evenly golden brown. Cool slightly. Cut into squares to serve.

PER SERVING *(1 square each)* **CAL** 109, **FAT** 4 g *(1 g sat. fat)*, **CHOL** 2 mg, **SODIUM** 236 mg, **CARB** 15 g *(2 g fiber, 0 g sugars)*, **PRO** 3 g

Florentine Feta Rolls

17g
CARB

SERVES 12
HANDS ON 25 min.
TOTAL 45 min.

- ⅓ cup finely chopped green onions
- ¼ cup chopped fresh basil
- 2 cloves garlic, minced
- 2 Tbsp. olive oil
- 1 10-oz. pkg. frozen chopped spinach, thawed and squeezed dry
- ¼ tsp. black pepper
- 1 13.8-oz. pkg. refrigerated pizza dough
- ¼ cup crumbled feta cheese (1 oz.)
- 2 Tbsp. toasted pine nuts
- 1 Tbsp. butter, melted

1. Preheat oven to 400°F. Grease the bottom of a 13×9-inch baking pan. In a large skillet cook and stir onions, basil, and garlic in 1 Tbsp. of the olive oil over medium 1 to 2 minutes or until basil is wilted and onions are tender. Remove from heat. Stir in spinach and pepper.
2. On a well-floured surface unroll pizza dough and shape into a 12×8-inch rectangle. Brush surface of dough with the remaining 1 Tbsp. olive oil. Spread spinach mixture to within 1 inch of the edges of dough. Sprinkle with feta cheese and pine nuts. Starting from a long side, roll up rectangle into a spiral. Pinch dough to seal seams. Slice roll into 12 pieces. Arrange pieces in the prepared pan. Brush with melted butter.
3. Bake 18 to 20 minutes or until golden brown. Let stand in pan on a wire rack 2 minutes. Remove rolls from pan; serve warm.

PER SERVING *(1 roll each)* **CAL** 138, **FAT** 6 g *(2 g sat. fat)*, **CHOL** 5 mg, **SODIUM** 309 mg, **CARB** 17 g *(1 g fiber, 2 g sugars)*, **PRO** 4 g

Cracked Black Pepper and Rosemary Focaccia

15g
CARB

SERVES 16
HANDS ON 15 min.
TOTAL 1 hr. 50 min.

- 1¼ cups all-purpose flour
- 1 pkg. active dry yeast
- 1 tsp. kosher salt
- 1 cup warm water (120°F to 130°F)
- 3 Tbsp. olive oil
- 1¼ to 1½ cups whole wheat flour
- 2 cloves garlic, thinly sliced
- ½ cup pitted Kalamata or ripe olives, halved or sliced (optional)
- 1 tsp. chopped fresh rosemary or ½ tsp. dried rosemary, crushed
- ½ tsp. cracked black pepper
- ½ cup finely shredded Parmesan cheese (2 oz.)

1. In a large bowl combine all-purpose flour, yeast, and ½ tsp. of the salt; add the warm water and 2 Tbsp. of the olive oil. Beat with an mixer on low 30 seconds, scraping sides of bowl constantly. Beat on high 3 minutes. Using a wooden spoon, stir in as much of the whole wheat flour as you can.
2. Turn dough out onto a lightly floured surface. Knead in enough of the remaining whole wheat flour to make a moderately stiff dough that is smooth and elastic (3 to 4 minutes total).
3. Place dough in a lightly oiled bowl, turning once to coat surface. Cover and let rise in a warm place 30 minutes. Punch dough down. Let rest 10 minutes. Place dough on a large greased or parchment-lined baking sheet. Press dough into a 13×9-inch rectangle.
4. Brush the remaining 1 Tbsp. olive oil evenly over dough. Sprinkle with garlic, olives (if desired), rosemary, the remaining ½ tsp. salt, the cracked black pepper, and cheese. Cover and

Florentine
Feta Rolls

Honey-
Oatmeal
Bread

Honey-Oatmeal Bread

25g **CARB**

SERVES	30
HANDS ON	20 min.
TOTAL	3 hr. 30 min.

- 4½ cups all-purpose flour
- 2 cups muesli
- 1 cup chopped nuts or snipped dried fruit (optional)
- 4 tsp. kosher salt
- 1 pkg. active dry yeast
- 2¾ cups warm water (120°F to 130°F)
- ⅔ Tbsp. honey
- 2 Tbsp. vegetable oil
- Cornmeal
- All-purpose flour

1. In an extra-large bowl combine the 4½ cups flour, the muesli, nuts or fruit (if desired), salt, and yeast. In a glass measuring cup stir together the water, honey, and oil; add to the flour mixture. Stir until moistened (dough will be very sticky and soft). Cover loosely with plastic wrap. Let stand at room temperature 2 hours.

2. For each loaf, grease a large or extra-large cast-iron skillet or baking sheet. Dust generously with cornmeal. Do not punch dough down. With well-floured hands, transfer dough portion to a well-floured surface; lightly flour top. Score dough into thirds with a knife. Shape portions into balls by gently pulling and tucking edges under. Place balls in prepared skillet or on baking sheet. Sprinkle lightly with flour. Cover loosely with plastic wrap. Let rise in a warm place 20 minutes.

3. Preheat oven to 450°F. Using a sharp knife, score bread tops. Place on rack in middle of oven. Place a shallow pan with 2 cups hot tap water on the rack below. Bake 25 to 30 minutes or until crust is deep golden brown. Transfer loaves to a wire rack; cool completely.

TIP If desired, transfer dough to a plastic container with a loose-fitting lid. Store in the refrigerator up to 7 days. If desired, bake dough portions on different days. If using chilled dough, increase rising time in Step 2 to 45 minutes. The dough becomes stickier the longer it chills. Take care not to overwork the sticky dough; you don't want to eliminate air pockets that have formed.

PER SERVING *(1 slice each)* **CAL** 121, **FAT** 1 g *(0 g sat. fat)*, **CHOL** 0 mg, **SODIUM** 227 mg, **CARB** 25 g *(1 g fiber, 0 g sugars)*, **PRO** 3 g

Pumpkin Seed Breadsticks

Pumpkin Seed Breadsticks

6g **CARB**

SERVES	24
HANDS ON	15 min.
TOTAL	30 min.

- 1 13.8-oz. pkg. refrigerated pizza dough
- 1 egg, lightly beaten
- 2 to 3 Tbsp. pumpkin seeds, coarsely chopped
- Coarse salt or salt

1. Preheat oven to 425°F. Lightly grease two large baking sheets. Unroll pizza dough on a lightly floured surface. Shape dough into a 12×9-inch rectangle. Brush with some of the egg. Sprinkle with pumpkin seeds and lightly sprinkle with salt. Using a floured long knife or pizza cutter, cut dough crosswise into ¼- to ½-inch-wide strips.

2. Place strips on prepared baking sheets. Bake one sheet at a time 8 to 10 minutes or until golden. Transfer to a wire rack; cool.

PER SERVING *(1 breadstick each)* **CAL** 39, **FAT** 1 g *(0 g sat. fat)*, **CHOL** 9 mg, **SODIUM** 75 mg, **CARB** 6 g *(0 g fiber, 0 g sugars)*, **PRO** 1 g

No-Knead
Honey
Bread

SAME DAY BREAD

Prepare as directed in Step 1,
except omit chilling dough.
Let dough stand in bowl, covered,
at room temperature 30 minutes.
Continue as directed in Step 2.
The bread will still taste great,
but it will spread a little more
and won't rise as high
as bread that has
been chilled.

No-Knead Honey Bread

26g CARB

SERVES 12
HANDS ON 25 min.
TOTAL 6 hr. 30 min.

- ¾ cup warm water (105°F to 115°F)
- 1 pkg. active dry yeast
- ⅓ cup milk
- 2 Tbsp. honey
- 2 Tbsp. butter or olive oil
- 1½ tsp. salt
- 2¾ cups all-purpose flour
  Nonstick cooking spray
  Cornmeal
- 1 egg white
- 2 tsp. water
  Fresh thyme, sage, oregano, and/or Italian parsley sprigs

1. In a large mixing bowl stir together the ¾ cup water and the yeast. Let stand 5 minutes. Meanwhile, in a small saucepan heat and stir milk, honey, butter, and salt just until warm (120°F to 130°F) and butter almost melts. Stir milk mixture into yeast mixture until combined. Stir in flour (dough will be sticky). Lightly coat a medium bowl with cooking spray; transfer dough to the greased bowl. Lightly coat a sheet of plastic wrap with cooking spray; cover bowl with the greased plastic wrap, coated side down. Chill at least 4 hours or up to 24 hours.

2. Using a dough scraper or spatula, carefully loosen dough from bowl and turn out onto a floured surface. Cover with greased plastic wrap. Let stand 30 minutes.

3. Lightly coat a baking sheet with cooking spray; sprinkle lightly with cornmeal. Gently shape dough into an 8- to 9-inch oval loaf, lightly flouring dough as needed. Transfer loaf to the prepared baking sheet. Cover with a clean kitchen towel and place on the middle rack of an unheated oven; place a bowl of warm water on the lower rack. Let rise until nearly double in size (about 1 hour).

4. Remove loaf from oven; uncover. Preheat oven to 400°F. In a small bowl whisk together egg white and the 2 tsp. water; brush over loaf. Arrange herbs on loaf. Brush herbs with egg mixture.

5. Bake 23 to 25 minutes or until temperature in center of loaf registers 200°F. Transfer to a wire rack; let cool.

PER SERVING (1 slice each) **CAL** 142, **FAT** 2 g (1 g sat. fat), **CHOL** 6 mg, **SODIUM** 315 mg, **CARB** 26 g (1 g fiber, 3 g sugars), **PRO** 4 g

Peppery Shallot Scone Bites

Peppery Shallot Scone Bites

17g CARB

SERVES 9
HANDS ON 20 min.
TOTAL 35 min.

- ¾ cup all-purpose flour
- ¾ cup whole wheat pastry flour or whole wheat flour
- 2 tsp. baking powder
- ¼ tsp. cream of tartar
- ¼ tsp. salt
- ¼ tsp. freshly ground black pepper
- ¼ cup light stick butter (not margarine)
- 2 Tbsp. butter
- ⅓ cup thinly sliced green onion tops
- ½ cup fat-free milk
- 9 very thin shallot slices
  Olive oil nonstick cooking spray

1. Preheat oven to 450°F. In a medium bowl stir together the first six ingredients (through pepper). Using a pastry blender, cut in light butter and butter until mixture resembles coarse crumbs. Stir in green onion tops. Make a well in the center of the flour mixture. Add milk to flour mixture. Using a fork, stir just until moistened.

2. Turn dough out onto a lightly floured surface. Knead dough by folding and gently pressing it four to six strokes or until dough is nearly smooth. Pat or lightly roll dough into a 7-inch square. Cut dough into nine squares. Place one shallot slice on top of each square. Coat the tops of the shallot slices with cooking spray and sprinkle with additional freshly ground pepper. Place squares 1 inch apart on an ungreased baking sheet.

3. Bake 12 to 14 minutes or until lightly browned. Remove scones from baking sheet; serve warm.

PER SERVING (1 scone each) **CAL** 128, **FAT** 6 g (3 g sat. fat), **CHOL** 14 mg, **SODIUM** 219 mg, **CARB** 17 g (2 g fiber, 1 g sugars), **PRO** 3 g

Cinnamon-Ginger Spiced Pear Muffins

Cinnamon-Ginger Spiced Pear Muffins

20g **CARB**

SERVES	18
HANDS ON	20 min.
TOTAL	1 hr.

Nonstick cooking spray
- 1 cup all-purpose flour
- ½ cup whole wheat flour
- 1½ tsp. baking powder
- 1 tsp. ground cinnamon
- ½ tsp. baking soda
- ½ tsp. ground ginger
- ¼ tsp. salt
- ¼ tsp. ground nutmeg
- 1 egg, lightly beaten
- 1 cup buttermilk
- ⅔ cup packed brown sugar
- ⅓ cup canola oil
- 2 tsp. vanilla
- 2 medium pears, peeled and cored
- 2 tsp. lemon juice
- 1 tsp. powdered sugar

1. Preheat oven to 400°F. Coat eighteen 2½-inch muffin cups with cooking spray. In a medium bowl combine the next eight ingredients (through nutmeg). Make a well in center of mixture.

2. In a small bowl combine the next five ingredients (through vanilla). Add to flour mixture; stir just until moistened.

3. Cut 18 thin slices from pears; brush with lemon juice. Chop the remaining pear and fold into batter. Spoon batter into prepared muffin cups. Top with pear slices.

4. Bake on separate oven racks 18 to 20 minutes or until a toothpick inserted in centers comes out clean, switching positions of pans halfway through baking. Immediately remove muffins from cups; cool on wire racks. Dust with powdered sugar.

PER SERVING *(1 muffin each)* **CAL** 127, **FAT** 5 g *(1 g sat. fat)*, **CHOL** 11 mg, **SODIUM** 129 mg, **CARB** 20 g *(1 g fiber, 11 g sugars)*, **PRO** 2 g

Bran Cereal Muffins

Bran Cereal Muffins

29g **CARB**

SERVES	24
HANDS ON	15 min.
TOTAL	40 min.

- 3 cups whole bran cereal (not flakes)
- 1 cup boiling water
- 2½ cups all-purpose flour
- ½ cup granulated sugar
- ½ cup packed brown sugar
- 2 tsp. baking powder
- 1 tsp. ground cinnamon (optional)
- ½ tsp. baking soda
- ½ tsp. salt
- 2 eggs, lightly beaten
- 2 cups buttermilk
- ½ cup vegetable oil

1. Preheat oven to 400°F. Grease twenty-four 2½-inch muffin cups or line with paper bake cups. In a medium bowl stir together cereal and the boiling water until moistened.

2. In another medium bowl stir together next seven ingredients (through salt). In a large bowl combine eggs, buttermilk, and oil. Stir cereal and flour mixture into egg mixture just until moistened. Spoon batter into the prepared muffin cups, filling cups three-fourths full.

3. Bake about 20 minutes or until a toothpick inserted in centers comes out clean. Cool in pan on a wire rack 5 minutes. Remove from muffin cups; serve warm.

TO MAKE AHEAD This batter can be made ahead and refrigerated up to 3 days. Bake chilled batter 20 to 22 minutes.

PER SERVING *(1 muffin each)* **CAL** 162, **FAT** 5 g *(1 g sat. fat)*, **CHOL** 18 mg, **SODIUM** 201 mg, **CARB** 29 g *(5 g fiber, 13 g sugars)*, **PRO** 3 g

Pour batter into prepared pans; spread evenly.

3. Bake 55 to 60 minutes for the 9×5-inch loaves, 45 to 50 minutes for the 8×4-inch loaves, or until a toothpick inserted near centers comes out clean.

4. Cool in pans on wire racks 10 minutes. Remove from pans; remove parchment. Cool completely on wire racks. For easier slicing, wrap in foil and store overnight before slicing.

PER SERVING (1 slice each) **CAL** 180, **FAT** 9 g (1 g sat. fat), **CHOL** 23 mg, **SODIUM** 173 mg, **CARB** 24 g (1 g fiber, 14 g sugars), **PRO** 3 g

Apple-Sunflower Pumpkin Bread

Apple Carrot Cake Muffins

23g
CARB

SERVES 24
HANDS ON 25 min.
TOTAL 55 min.

- 2 cups all-purpose flour
- 1¼ cups sugar
- 2 tsp. baking soda
- 1 to 1½ tsp. apple pie spice
- ½ tsp. salt
- 2 cups finely shredded carrots
- 1 cup shredded, peeled apple
- ½ cup raisins
- 3 eggs, lightly beaten
- ⅔ cup vegetable oil
- ⅓ cup milk
- 1 tsp. vanilla
- 1 recipe Coconut Streusel (right) (optional)

1. Preheat oven to 350°F. Grease twenty-four 2½-inch muffin cups or line with paper bake cups.

2. In a large bowl combine the first five ingredients (through salt). Make a well in center of flour mixture. In another bowl combine carrots, apple, and raisins. In a medium bowl combine eggs, oil, milk, and vanilla. Stir in carrot mixture. Add egg mixture to the flour mixture. Stir just until moistened (batter should be lumpy).

3. Spoon batter into prepared cups, filling each about three-fourths full. If desired, top with Coconut Streusel.

4. Bake 20 to 25 minutes or until golden. Cool 10 minutes in muffin cups. Remove muffins; serve warm or cool completely.

PER SERVING (1 muffin each) **CAL** 161, **FAT** 7 g (1 g sat. fat), **CHOL** 24 mg, **SODIUM** 172 mg, **CARB** 23 g (1 g fiber, 14 g sugars), **PRO** 2 g

Apple-Sunflower Pumpkin Bread

24g
CARB

SERVES 32
HANDS ON 30 min.
TOTAL 1 hr. 35 min.

Nonstick cooking spray
- 1½ cups whole wheat flour or white whole wheat flour
- 1½ cups all-purpose flour
- 2¼ tsp. pumpkin pie spice or 1½ tsp. ground cinnamon, ½ tsp. ground nutmeg, ¼ tsp. ground ginger, and ⅛ tsp. ground cloves
- 2 tsp. baking soda
- 1 tsp. salt
- 1 cup granulated sugar
- 1 cup packed brown sugar
- 1 cup walnut oil or vegetable oil
- 4 eggs
- ½ cup boiled cider, applejack, apple brandy, apple cider or apple juice
- 1 15-oz. can pumpkin

- 1½ cups finely chopped, peeled firm, sweet apples (such as Golden Delicious, Jonagold, Pink Lady, Braeburn, and/or Cameo)
- ½ cup dry-roasted sunflower seeds or chopped walnuts

1. Preheat oven to 350°F. Grease the bottom and ½ inch up sides of two 9×5-inch or three 8×4-inch loaf pans. Line bottoms with parchment paper; lightly coat parchment with cooking spray. In a large bowl combine the next five ingredients (through salt).

2. In an extra-large mixing bowl combine granulated sugar, brown sugar, and oil. Beat with a mixer on medium until well mixed. Add eggs; beat well. Alternately add flour mixture and boiled cider to sugar mixture, beating on low after each addition just until combined. Beat in pumpkin. Fold in apples and sunflower seeds.

Apple
Carrot
Cake
Muffins

COCONUT STREUSEL

In a bowl combine ¼ cup each all-purpose flour and packed brown sugar. Using a pastry blender, cut in ¼ cup cold butter, cut up. Stir in ½ cup shredded coconut.

Quick Seed Bread

Dilled Zucchini Bread

22g CARB

SERVES 28
HANDS ON 25 min.
TOTAL 3 hr. 20 min.

- 1½ cups all-purpose flour
- 1½ cups whole wheat flour
- 1 Tbsp. baking powder
- 1 tsp. salt
- 2 eggs, lightly beaten
- 2½ cups coarsely shredded unpeeled zucchini
- 1½ cups sugar
- 1 cup vegetable oil
- 1 tsp. vanilla
- 1 cup coarsely chopped walnuts or pecans
- ½ cup chopped fresh dill
  Fresh dill sprigs
  Walnut or pecan pieces
  Coarse sea salt or kosher salt

1. Preheat oven to 350°F. Grease bottom and ½ inch up sides of two 8×4-inch loaf pans. In a large bowl stir together the first four ingredients (through 1 tsp. salt).
2. In a medium bowl combine the next five ingredients (through vanilla). Make a well in center of flour mixture. Add zucchini mixture to flour mixture. Stir just until moistened (batter should be lumpy). Fold in the 1 cup nuts and chopped dill. Pour batter into prepared pans, spreading evenly. Arrange dill sprigs and nut pieces on top of batter and sprinkle with coarse salt.
3. Bake about 55 minutes or until a toothpick inserted in centers comes out clean. Cool in pans 15 minutes. Remove loaves from pans; cool on a wire rack. Wrap loaves in plastic wrap and store overnight at room temperature before slicing.

PER SERVING (1 slice each) **CAL** 195, **FAT** 11 g (1 g sat. fat), **CHOL** 13 mg, **SODIUM** 163 mg, **CARB** 22 g (1 g fiber, 11 g sugars), **PRO** 3 g

Quick Seed Bread

28g CARB

SERVES 14
HANDS ON 20 min.
TOTAL 1 hr. 15 min.

- 1½ cups all-purpose flour
- ½ cup whole wheat flour
- ¾ cup packed brown sugar
- ½ cup dry-roasted sunflower kernels
- ⅓ cup flaxseed meal
- 2 Tbsp. sesame seeds
- 2 Tbsp. poppy seeds
- 1 tsp. baking powder
- ½ tsp. baking soda
- ½ tsp. salt
- 1 egg
- 1¼ cups buttermilk or sour milk
- ¼ cup vegetable oil
- 4 tsp. sesame seeds, poppy seeds, and/or dry-roasted sunflower kernels

1. Preheat oven to 350°F. Grease the bottom and ½ inch up sides of a 9×5-inch loaf pan.
2. In a large bowl stir together the first 10 ingredients (through salt). Make a well in center of the flour mixture. In a medium bowl beat egg with a fork; stir in buttermilk and oil. Add egg mixture to flour mixture. Stir just until moistened (batter should be lumpy). Spread batter in the prepared pan. Sprinkle with the 4 tsp. seeds.
3. Bake 45 to 55 minutes or until a toothpick inserted near center comes out clean. Cool in pan on a wire rack 10 minutes. Remove from pan. Cool completely on wire rack. Wrap bread in plastic wrap and store overnight at room temperature before slicing.

TIP To make sour milk, add 1 Tbsp. lemon juice or vinegar to a liquid measuring cup. Add enough milk to make 1¼ cups total liquid. Stir; let stand 5 minutes before using.

PER SERVING (1 slice each) **CAL** 216, **FAT** 10 g (1 g sat. fat), **CHOL** 16 mg, **SODIUM** 180 mg, **CARB** 28 g (2 g fiber, 0 g sugars), **PRO** 5 g

Dilled
Zucchini
Bread

7

FESTIVE
ENDINGS

Yes, you may have dessert! Pie, cake, bars,
cookies, and bread pudding . . . they're all here,
ready to fill your kitchen with such time-
honored scents as pumpkin, ginger,
peppermint, cinnamon, and chocolate. Smaller
portions, less sugar and fat, and more
nutrient-dense ingredients make them a
healthier way to serve these treasured sweets.

138

145

150

Hasselback Pear Cake

TIP

To ensure you don't cut all the way through pear halves when slicing them into hasselbacks, lay chopsticks or skewers along both short sides. Cut down to the chopsticks.

Hasselback Pear Cake

42g CARB

SERVES 12
HANDS ON 20 min.
TOTAL 1 hr. 40 min.

- 2 firm, ripe Bartlett pears
- 1 cup granulated sugar
- 1 Tbsp. + 2 tsp. ground cinnamon
- ⅓ cup canola oil
- ⅓ cup applesauce
- 3 large eggs
- 1 Tbsp. vanilla extract
- 2 cups all-purpose flour
- 1½ cups almond flour
- 1 Tbsp. baking powder
- ½ tsp. salt
- ½ tsp. ground nutmeg
- ¼ tsp. ground cloves
- ¾ cup whipped cream (optional)

1. Preheat oven to 375°F. Coat a 9-inch springform pan with cooking spray.
2. Peel pears; cut in half lengthwise and remove cores. Place pear halves, cut sides down, on a cutting board. Make lengthwise slices across pear halves, cutting nearly through but leaving pears attached on flat sides.
3. In a small bowl stir together ⅓ cup of the sugar and 2 tsp. of the cinnamon. Set aside 2 Tbsp. of the mixture.
4. In another bowl whisk together the remaining ⅔ cup sugar and 1 Tbsp. cinnamon, the oil, and applesauce. Whisk in eggs and vanilla until combined. The mixture will be very dark and loose.
5. In a third bowl whisk together the next six ingredients (through cloves). Add flour mixture to the egg mixture. Using a rubber scraper, fold them together just until combined.
6. Sprinkle the reserved 2 Tbsp. cinnamon-sugar mixture in the bottom of the springform pan. Pour batter into pan, spreading evenly. Gently press pear halves about halfway into batter with the flat sides down and the necks of the pears toward the center. Be careful not to let pears touch pan sides. Sprinkle the pears and batter with the remaining cinnamon-sugar mixture.
7. Bake about 30 minutes or until a toothpick inserted in the center comes out clean. Cool in pan on a wire rack 15 minutes. Run a knife around the edge of cake and release the pan sides. Let cake cool 30 minutes more. Remove the pan bottom and transfer the cake to a serving plate. Cut into

Pumpkin-Walnut Baby Cakes

12 slices. If desired, top each serving with 1 Tbsp. whipped cream.

PER SERVING *(1 slice each)* **CAL** 320, **FAT** 15 g *(1 g sat. fat)*, **CHOL** 47 mg, **SODIUM** 243 mg, **CARB** 42 g *(4 g fiber, 21 g sugars)*, **PRO** 7 g

---

Pumpkin-Walnut Baby Cakes

30g CARB

SERVES 12
HANDS ON 25 min.
TOTAL 45 min.

- Nonstick cooking spray
- 1¼ cups brown rice flour
- ⅓ cup quick-cooking rolled oats
- ¼ cup flaxseed meal
- 2 tsp. pumpkin pie spice
- 1½ tsp. baking powder
- ½ tsp. salt
- 2 eggs, lightly beaten
- ¾ cup canned pumpkin
- ½ cup packed brown sugar
- ½ cup milk
- 3 Tbsp. canola oil
- 1 tsp. vanilla
- ¼ cup chopped walnuts
- 2 Tbsp. quick-cooking rolled oats
- 1 Tbsp. packed brown sugar
- 1 Tbsp. canola oil
- 1 recipe Cream Cheese Drizzle (optional)

1. Preheat oven to 375°F. Coat twelve 2½-inch muffin cups with cooking spray (do not use paper bake cups). In a medium bowl stir together next six ingredients (through salt). Make a well in center of mixture.
2. In another bowl combine next six ingredients (through vanilla). Add to flour mixture. Stir just until moistened (batter should be lumpy). Spoon batter into prepared muffin cups.
3. In a small bowl combine next four ingredients (through oil). Sprinkle over batter in muffin cups.
4. Bake about 15 minutes or until a toothpick inserted in centers comes out clean. Cool in cups on a wire rack 5 minutes. Remove from cups; cool slightly. If desired, drizzle baby cakes with Cream Cheese Drizzle. Serve warm

CREAM CHEESE DRIZZLE In a small bowl stir together 1 oz. softened reduced-fat cream cheese (neufchatel) and 2 Tbsp. powdered sugar until smooth. Gradually stir 1 to 2 tbsp. milk to reach drizzling consistency.

PER SERVING *(1 cake each)* **CAL** 216, **FAT** 9 g *(1 g sat. fat)*, **CHOL** 34 mg, **SODIUM** 188 mg, **CARB** 30 g *(2 g fiber, 13 g sugars)*, **PRO** 4 g

Apple-
Cranberry
Gingerbread
Upside-Down
Cake

Apple-Cranberry Gingerbread Upside-Down Cake

26g
CARB

SERVES 16	
HANDS ON 30 min.	
TOTAL 1 hr. 50 min.	

- ¼ cup pure maple syrup
- 2 Tbsp. light stick butter, melted
- 2 tsp. apple pie spice
- ⅔ cup fresh or frozen, thawed cranberries, chopped
- 1⅓ cups chopped cooking apple
- 2 cups all-purpose flour
- 1 tsp. baking powder
- ¼ tsp. baking soda
- ¼ tsp. salt
- ¾ cup water
- ½ cup refrigerated or frozen egg product, thawed, or 2 eggs
- ⅓ cup canola oil
- ¼ cup molasses
- ¼ cup packed brown sugar

1. Preheat oven to 325°F. Grease a 10-inch fluted tube pan. In a bowl combine syrup, butter, and 1 tsp. of the apple pie spice. Pour into the prepared pan. Add cranberries and apple, spreading evenly.

2. In a bowl combine the remaining 1 tsp. apple pie spice and the next four ingredients (through salt). In another bowl whisk together the next five ingredients (through brown sugar). Add egg mixture to flour mixture. Stir until well combined. Slowly pour over fruit in pan.

3. Bake 40 to 45 minutes or until a toothpick inserted in center comes out clean. Cool in pan 10 minutes. Invert cake onto a cake platter. Cool about 30 minutes. Serve warm.

PER SERVING *(1 slice each)* **CAL** 159, **FAT** 6 g *(1 g sat. fat)*, **CHOL** 2 mg, **SODIUM** 118 mg, **CARB** 26 g *(1 g fiber, 12 g sugars)*, **PRO** 2 g

Peppermint Chocolate Tart

21g
CARB

SERVES 12	
HANDS ON 20 min.	
TOTAL 4 hr. 20 min.	

- ½ cup + 2 Tbsp. all-purpose flour
- ½ cup + 1 Tbsp. white whole wheat flour
- ½ tsp. ground cinnamon
- ¼ tsp. salt
- ¼ cup canola oil

- 3 Tbsp. ice water
- 8 oz. bittersweet chocolate chips (60% cacao)
- 1 cup fat-free milk
- 1 Tbsp. cornstarch
- 1 tsp. peppermint extract
- ¼ tsp. salt
- 1 peppermint candy
- ¾ cup whipped cream (optional)

1. Preheat oven to 350°F. Place water in freezer to cool while you make the dough.

2. In a medium bowl whisk together flours, cinnamon, and salt. Drizzle with oil and toss with a fork until evenly damp and crumbly. Drizzle with ice water; toss with the fork. Use your hands to form dough into a ball, but don't knead or overwork it.

3. Place the dough between two large pieces of waxed paper. Roll dough into an 11-inch circle. Remove top piece of waxed paper; carefully invert dough circle into a 9-inch tart pan with a removable bottom. Gently press dough into bottom and up sides of pan. Trim and patch where necessary. Prick bottom of crust all over with a fork.

4. Place pan in center of oven. Bake about 20 minutes or until dough pulls away slightly from edges. Cool completely on a wire rack.

5. For filling, place chocolate chips in a medium bowl. In a 2-qt. saucepan combine milk and cornstarch. Bring to boiling over medium-high; cook about 5 minutes or until the mixture looks thick like honey and frothy, whisking constantly. Pour over chocolate chips. Add peppermint extract and salt; let stand 1 minute without stirring. After 1 minute, stir gently with a rubber scraper until chocolate is melted and mixture is thick like pudding. Press a piece of plastic wrap directly on surface of filling. Let stand at room temperature 20 minutes.

6. Pour filling into cooled crust. Gently swirl the surface of the chocolate using the back of a spoon. Refrigerate, uncovered, 4 hours.

7. If desired, crush peppermint candy and sprinkle over the tart. Use a hot knife to cut the tart into 12 pieces. If desired, top each piece with 1 Tbsp. whipped cream.

PER SERVING *(1 slice each)* **CAL** 194, **FAT** 12 g *(5 g sat. fat)*, **CHOL** 0 mg, **SODIUM** 106 mg, **CARB** 21 g *(2 g fiber, 9 g sugars)*, **PRO** 3 g

Peppermint
Chocolate
Tart

Cinnamon-
Sugar
Apple Pie
Bars

Cinnamon-Sugar Apple Pie Bars

26g CARB

SERVES 32
HANDS ON 40 min.
TOTAL 1 hr. 25 min.

- 3¾ cups all-purpose flour
- 2 Tbsp. sugar
- 1½ tsp. salt
- ¾ cup shortening
- ⅓ cup cold butter, cut up
- ⅔ to 1 cup ice water
- 8 cups thinly sliced, peeled tart cooking apples (8 to 10)
- 1¼ cups sugar
- 2 tsp. ground cinnamon
- 1 egg white
- 1 Tbsp. cold water

1. Preheat oven to 350°F. In a large bowl combine flour, the 2 Tbsp. sugar, and the salt. Using a pastry blender, cut in shortening and butter until pieces are pea size. Sprinkle 1 Tbsp. of the ice water over part of the flour mixture; toss gently with a fork. Push moistened dough to side of bowl. Repeat moistening flour mixture, using 1 Tbsp. of the ice water at a time, until all of the flour mixture is moistened. Shape two-thirds of the dough into a ball. Shape the remaining dough into a smaller ball.

2. Place the larger ball of dough between two pieces of lightly floured waxed paper. Roll dough into a 17×12-inch rectangle. Remove top piece of waxed paper. Carefully invert pastry into a 15×10-inch baking pan. Peel off waxed paper. Press dough up sides of pan; trim edges (if needed, use trimmed pieces to patch any holes). Top with thinly sliced apples.

3. In a small bowl combine the 1¼ cups sugar and the cinnamon. Set aside ⅓ cup of the cinnamon-sugar mixture. Sprinkle the remaining cinnamon-sugar mixture over apples.

4. Place the remaining dough between two pieces of lightly floured waxed paper; roll into a 16×11-inch rectangle. Remove top piece of waxed paper. Invert pastry over apple layer. Peel off waxed paper. Pinch or crimp edges of pastry together to seal. Cut slits in the top pastry. In a small bowl whisk together egg white and the 1 Tbsp. cold water; brush over pastry. Sprinkle reserved cinnamon-sugar mixture evenly over pastry.

5. Bake about 45 minutes or until pastry is golden brown and apples are tender. Cool in pan on a wire rack.

PER SERVING (1 bar each) **CAL** 171, **FAT** 7 g (2 g sat. fat), **CHOL** 5 mg, **SODIUM** 127 mg, **CARB** 26 g (2 g fiber, 13 g sugars), **PRO** 2 g

Caramel-Pear Bread Pudding

Caramel-Pear Bread Pudding

28g CARB

SERVES 12
HANDS ON 25 min.
TOTAL 1 hr. 45 min.

- Nonstick cooking spray
- 8 slices whole grain white bread or whole grain wheat bread, cut into ½-inch pieces and dried
- 2 Tbsp. tub-style vegetable oil spread, melted
- 2 large red-skin pears
- ¼ cup dried cranberries (optional)
- 2 cups fat-free milk
- ¾ cup refrigerated or frozen egg product, thawed, or 3 eggs, lightly beaten
- ⅔ cup sugar-free caramel ice cream topping
- ½ tsp. ground cinnamon
- ½ cup coarsely chopped pecans, toasted (optional)

1. Preheat oven to 350°F. Lightly coat a 2-qt. rectangular or square baking dish with cooking spray. In a large bowl toss together dried bread and melted vegetable oil spread until coated.

Core and chop one of the pears and add to the bread mixture along with the cranberries (if using). Gently toss to combine. Transfer to the prepared baking dish.

2. In a bowl whisk together milk, eggs, ⅓ cup of the caramel topping, and the cinnamon. Slowly pour milk mixture evenly over bread mixture in dish. Using the back of a spoon, gently press down on top of bread mixture.

3. Bake, uncovered, 50 to 60 minutes or until a knife inserted near center comes out clean. Let stand on a wire rack 30 minutes.

4. To serve, cut pudding into 12 portions and place on dessert plates. Quarter and core the remaining pear. Cut into very thin slices; place a few slices on top of each portion. If desired, sprinkle with pecans. Drizzle each serving with some of the remaining ⅓ cup caramel topping.

TIP To dry bread cubes, place in an ungreased 15×10-inch baking pan. Bake in a 300°F oven 10 to 12 minutes or until dry and crisp, stirring once or twice. You should have about 5 cups dried bread cubes.

TIP To toast nuts, spread in a shallow pan. Bake in a 350°F oven 5 to 10 minutes or until toasted, shaking pan once or twice.

PER SERVING (½ cup each) **CAL** 147, **FAT** 2 g (1 g sat. fat), **CHOL** 2 mg, **SODIUM** 169 mg, **CARB** 28 g (2 g fiber, 7 g sugars), **PRO** 5 g

Espresso Custards

Sweet Potato Brownies

22g CARB

SERVES 16
HANDS ON 20 min.
TOTAL 45 min.

- ½ cup coconut sugar or granulated sugar
- ⅓ cup all-purpose flour
- ⅓ cup unsweetened cocoa powder
- 1½ tsp. baking soda
- ⅛ tsp. salt
- 1 cup almond butter
- ¾ cup mashed cooked sweet potato
- ¼ cup honey
- 1 tsp. vanilla
- 3 oz. bittersweet chocolate, finely chopped

1. Preheat oven to 325°F. Line an 8-inch square baking pan with parchment paper. In a medium bowl stir together first five ingredients (through salt).
2. In a large bowl combine next four ingredients (through vanilla). Stir in flour mixture just until combined. Stir in chocolate. Spread batter in the prepared pan.
3. Bake 25 to 30 minutes or until top is puffed and appears dry. Cool in pan on a wire rack. If desired, dust with additional cocoa powder.

TIP For mashed sweet potato, peel one 8-oz. sweet potato and cut into 2-inch pieces. Place potato in a steamer basket in a saucepan. Add water to saucepan to just below basket. Bring to boiling; reduce heat. Steam, covered, about 18 minutes or until very tender. Press sweet potato through a ricer or mash with a potato masher.

PER SERVING (1 brownie each) **CAL** 190, **FAT** 11 g (2 g sat. fat), **CHOL** 0 mg, **SODIUM** 181 mg, **CARB** 22 g (3 g fiber, 14 g sugars), **PRO** 5 g

Espresso Custards

24g CARB

SERVES 4
HANDS ON 25 min.
TOTAL 4 hr. 40 min.

- 2 cups fat-free milk
- 1 envelope unflavored gelatin
- 3 egg yolks
- ⅓ cup sugar
- 1½ tsp. vanilla
- 1½ tsp. instant espresso coffee powder
  Chopped chocolate-covered espresso beans or whipped topping (optional)

1. In a small bowl sprinkle ¼ cup of the milk with gelatin. Let stand 5 minutes. Meanwhile, in a medium saucepan whisk together egg yolks and sugar. Gradually whisk in remaining 1¾ cups milk. Cook and stir over medium just until boiling. Remove from heat.

2. Gradually whisk about ½ cup of the hot mixture into gelatin mixture; return to remaining hot mixture in saucepan. Place saucepan in a large bowl of ice water. Add vanilla, stirring for a few minutes to cool custard. Transfer ½ cup of the custard to a small bowl; stir in espresso powder.
3. Pour remaining custard into four 6-oz. mugs, dessert bowls, or custard cups. Cover and chill 15 to 20 minutes. Drizzle with espresso custard; lightly swirl into top. Cover loosely and chill at least 4 hours or until set. If desired, top with espresso beans or whipped topping.

TIP If the custard is too firm to swirl, just drizzle the espresso mixture over custard and spread to cover the top.

PER SERVING (½ cup each) **CAL** 177, **FAT** 3 g (1 g sat. fat), **CHOL** 160 mg, **SODIUM** 72 mg, **CARB** 24 g (0 g fiber, 23 g sugars), **PRO** 12 g

Sweet
Potato
Brownies

Cinnamon
Bars

Cinnamon Bars

28g CARB

SERVES 24	
HANDS ON 20 min.	
TOTAL 45 min.	

- 2 cups all-purpose flour
- 3 tsp. ground cinnamon
- 1 tsp. baking powder
- ¼ tsp. baking soda
- 2 cups packed brown sugar
- ⅔ cup butter
- 2 eggs
- 2 tsp. vanilla
- ¼ cup granulated sugar
- 1 Tbsp. butter, melted

1. Preheat oven to 350°F. Line a 9-inch square baking pan with foil, extending the foil over edges of pan. Grease foil. In a medium bowl stir together flour, 2 tsp. of the cinnamon, the baking powder, and baking soda.

2. In a medium saucepan cook and stir brown sugar and the ⅔ cup butter over medium until butter melts and mixture is smooth. Remove from heat; cool slightly. Stir in eggs and vanilla. Stir in flour mixture until combined. Spread batter into the prepared baking pan.

3. Bake 25 to 30 minutes or until a toothpick inserted in center comes out clean. Cool slightly in pan on a wire rack.

4. In a small bowl stir together granulated sugar and the remaining 1 tsp. cinnamon. Brush warm bars with the 1 Tbsp. melted butter and sprinkle with cinnamon-sugar mixture; cool completely. Using the edges of the foil, lift uncut bars from pan. Cut into bars.

TO STORE Layer bars between sheets of waxed paper in an airtight container; cover. Store at room temperature up to 3 days or freeze up to 1 month.

PER SERVING (1 bar each) **CAL** 131, **FAT** 1 g (1 g sat. fat), **CHOL** 18 mg, **SODIUM** 52 mg, **CARB** 28 g (0 g fiber, 20 g sugars), **PRO** 2 g

Cranberry Crumble Bars

Cranberry Crumble Bars

27g CARB

SERVES 15	
HANDS ON 25 min.	
TOTAL 1 hr. 20 min.	

- 1 orange
- 2 cups cranberries
- 6 Tbsp. granulated sugar
- 1½ Tbsp. cornstarch
- 2 tsp. almond extract
- ¼ tsp. ground cinnamon
- 1½ cups all-purpose flour
- 1½ cups almond flour
- ½ cup granulated sugar
- 1 tsp. baking powder
- ¼ tsp. salt
- ¼ tsp. ground nutmeg
- 4 Tbsp. cold unsalted butter, cubed
- 2 large egg whites
- 1½ tsp. vanilla extract
- 2 tsp. powdered sugar (optional)

1. Preheat oven to 375°F. Line a 13×9-inch baking pan with foil, extending foil over edges of pan. Coat foil with cooking spray. Remove zest from orange; squeeze juice from half of the orange.

2. For filling, in a bowl stir together half of the orange zest, the orange juice, and the next five ingredients (through cinnamon).

3. For crust, in a medium bowl whisk together the remaining orange zest and the next six ingredients (through nutmeg). Use your hands to pinch and rub butter into flour mixture until the pieces are flattened and the mixture is crumbly and resembles sand.

4. In a small bowl lightly beat egg whites and vanilla with a fork. Add flour mixture; stir with fork until well incorporated. Set aside ½ cup of the mixture. Press the remaining flour mixture over bottom of the prepared baking pan.

5. Stir filling, then pour it over crust in pan, spreading evenly. Sprinkle the reserved crust mixture over top.

6. Bake about 40 minutes or until lightly browned. Cool in pan on a wire rack 15 minutes. Use foil to lift uncut bars out of pan; cut into bars. Cool completely. If desired, sprinkle bars with powdered sugar before serving.

PER SERVING (1 bar each) **CAL** 199, **FAT** 9 g (2 g sat. fat), **CHOL** 8 mg, **SODIUM** 84 mg, **CARB** 27 g (2 g fiber, 13 g sugars), **PRO** 4 g

Chocolate-Date Truffles

19g
CARB

SERVES	10
HANDS ON	30 min.
TOTAL	1 hr. 30 min.

- ½ cup coarsely chopped walnuts
- ⅛ tsp. salt
- 1½ cups pitted whole Medjool dates
- 3 Tbsp. unsweetened cocoa powder
- 1 Tbsp. apple juice
- ¼ tsp. salt
- 3 to 4 tsp. water (optional)

1. In a food processor combine walnuts and the ⅛ tsp. salt. Cover and pulse until finely chopped. Transfer to a shallow dish.

2. In food processor combine the next four ingredients (through ¼ tsp. salt). Cover and process until mixture forms a thick paste, adding water, 1 tsp. at a time, if needed.

3. Using 2 tsp. of the dough for each truffle, shape into balls. Roll balls in walnuts to coat. (If dough is too sticky, chill 15 to 20 minutes.) If desired, dust with additional cocoa powder. Cover and chill at least 1 hour before serving.

TO STORE Layer truffles between sheets of waxed paper in an airtight container. Store in the refrigerator up to 2 weeks.

PER SERVING *(2 truffles each)* **CAL** 105, **FAT** 4 g *(0 g sat. fat)*, **CHOL** 0 mg, **SODIUM** 88 mg, **CARB** 19 g *(2 g fiber, 15 g sugars)*, **PRO** 2 g

Pumpkin Pie Tassies

12g
CARB

SERVES	24
HANDS ON	30 min.
TOTAL	1 hr. 5 min.

1 **14.1-oz. pkg. (2 crusts) rolled
  refrigerated unbaked piecrust
  Nonstick cooking spray**
¾ **cup canned pumpkin**
¼ **cup granulated sugar**
1 **tsp. pumpkin pie spice**
⅛ **tsp. salt**
1 **egg, lightly beaten**
¼ **cup half-and-half or milk**
⅓ **cup chopped pecans**
1 **Tbsp. packed brown sugar**
1 **Tbsp. butter, melted**
  Maple syrup (optional)

1. Let piecrusts stand according to package directions. Preheat oven to 350°F. Coat twenty-four 1¾-inch muffin cups with cooking spray. Unroll piecrusts. Using a 2½-inch round cookie cutter, cut 12 rounds from each piecrust. Gently press pastry rounds onto bottoms and up sides of the prepared muffin cups.

2. For filling, in a large bowl stir together next four ingredients (through salt). Stir in egg and half-and-half just until combined. For topping, in a small bowl stir together pecans, brown sugar, and melted butter.

3. Spoon about 2 tsp. filling into each pastry-lined muffin cup. Top each with about 1 tsp. topping.

4. Bake about 30 minutes or until filling is set and pastry is golden brown. Cool in muffin cups on a wire rack 5 minutes. Remove from muffin cups; cool on wire rack. If desired, drizzle tassies with maple syrup before serving.

TO STORE Place tassies in a single layer in an airtight container. Store in the refrigerator up to 2 days or freeze up to 3 months.

PER SERVING *(1 tassie each)* **CAL** 101,
FAT 6 g *(2 g sat. fat)*, **CHOL** 12 mg,
SODIUM 107 mg, **CARB** 12 g *(0 g fiber, 3 g sugars)*,
PRO 1 g

Rocky
Road
Cookie
Cups

Cherry-
Almond
Cookie
Cups

Lemon
Fluff
Cookie
Cups

Sugar Cookie Cups

8g CARB

SERVES 64
HANDS ON 1 hr.
TOTAL 1 hr. 15 min.

Nonstick cooking spray
- 1 cup butter, softened
- 1¼ cups sugar
- 1½ tsp. baking powder
- ½ tsp. salt
- 2 eggs
- 2 tsp. vanilla
- 1 tsp. orange zest or almond extract (optional)
- 3 cups all-purpose flour

1. Coat 1¾-inch muffin cups with cooking spray. In a large bowl beat butter with a mixer on medium 30 seconds. Beat in sugar, baking powder, and salt, scraping sides of bowl as needed. Beat in eggs, vanilla, and, if desired, orange zest. Beat in as much of the flour as you can with the mixer. Stir in any remaining flour. If necessary, cover and chill dough about 30 minutes or until easy to handle.
2. Preheat oven to 350°F. Shape dough into 1¼-inch balls. Press dough balls into bottom and up sides of prepared muffin cups.
3. Bake 10 to 12 minutes or until edges are lightly browned. Repress cookie cup centers with the rounded side of a measuring spoon. Cool in pans 5 minutes. Remove cups from pans; cool completely on wire racks. Fill as desired from variations.

TO STORE Layer unfilled cookie cups between sheets of waxed paper in an airtight container; cover. Store at room temperature up to 3 days or freeze up to 3 months. Fill cookie cups just before serving.

PER SERVING *(1 cookie cup each)* **CAL** 65, **FAT** 3 g *(2 g sat. fat)*, **CHOL** 13 mg, **SODIUM** 55 mg, **CARB** 8 g *(0 g fiber, 4 g sugars)*, **PRO** 1 g

ROCKY ROAD COOKIE CUPS

Place one 13-oz. jar marshmallow creme in a resealable plastic bag; snip a small hole in one corner. Squeeze marshmallow creme into each cookie cup. Drizzle with chocolate ice cream topping; sprinkle with chopped peanuts.

PER SERVING *(1 cookie cup each)* **CAL** 93, **FAT** 3 g *(2 g sat. fat)*, **CHOL** 13 mg, **SODIUM** 63 mg, **CARB** 15 g *(0 g fiber, 8 g sugars)*, **PRO** 1 g

CHERRY-ALMOND COOKIE CUPS

Prepare cookie cups as directed, using the almond extract option. In a small bowl beat ½ cup heavy cream, 4 tsp. sour cream, 1 Tbsp. sugar, and ¼ tsp. vanilla with a mixer on medium until soft peaks form. Fill each cookie cup with 1 tsp. cherry preserves. Top with whipped cream mixture and toasted sliced almonds.

PER SERVING *(1 cookie cup each)* **CAL** 97, **FAT** 4 g *(2 g sat. fat)*, **CHOL** 16 mg, **SODIUM** 58 mg, **CARB** 14 g *(0 g fiber, 8 g sugars)*, **PRO** 1 g

LEMON FLUFF COOKIE CUPS

Place half of a 10-oz. jar lemon curd in a medium bowl; stir until smooth. In a separate bowl beat ½ cup heavy cream with 1 Tbsp. powdered sugar until soft peaks form. Gently fold whipped cream into lemon curd. Spoon or pipe into cups. Sprinkle with lemon, orange, and/or lime zest.

PER SERVING *(1 cookie cup each)* **CAL** 79, **FAT** 4 g *(2 g sat. fat)*, **CHOL** 17 mg, **SODIUM** 57 mg, **CARB** 10 g *(6 g fiber, 4 g sugars)*, **PRO** 1 g

CHOCOLATE-PEPPERMINT MOUSSE COOKIE CUPS

Fill a large bowl with ice and water. Place a slightly smaller bowl in the large bowl with ice water to make an ice bath. In a small saucepan heat and stir 6 oz. semisweet chocolate, chopped, and ½ cup water over medium until chocolate is melted. Remove from heat; stir in ½ tsp. vanilla and a few drops peppermint extract (mixture may appear grainy). Pour chocolate mixture into the smaller bowl in ice bath. Whisk 2 to 3 minutes or until thickened. Fold in one-fourth of an 8-oz. container frozen whipped dessert topping, thawed. Pipe or spoon filling into cups. If desired, sprinkle with crushed peppermint candies.

PER SERVING *(1 cookie cup each)* **CAL** 80, **FAT** 4 g *(2 g sat. fat)*, **CHOL** 13 mg, **SODIUM** 55 mg, **CARB** 10 g *(0 g fiber, 6 g sugars)*, **PRO** 1 g

Chocolate-Peppermint Mousse Cookie Cups

Rosemary-Almond Cookies

17g CARB

SERVES 42
HANDS ON 1 hr.
TOTAL 5 hr. 10 min.

- 1½ **cups sugar**
- ¾ **cup slivered almonds**
- 3 **Tbsp. fresh rosemary leaves**
- 1 **cup butter, softened**
- ½ **tsp. baking powder**
- ½ **tsp. salt**
- 2 **eggs**
- ¼ **cup milk**
- 2 **tsp. vanilla bean paste or vanilla**
- ½ **tsp. almond extract**
- 3 **cups all-purpose flour**
  Very small fresh rosemary sprigs (optional)
- 1 **recipe Almond Glaze**

1. In a small food processor or blender combine ½ cup of the sugar, the almonds, and rosemary leaves. Cover; pulse until nuts are finely ground (but not oily) and rosemary is pulverized.
2. In a large bowl beat butter with a mixer on medium to high 30 seconds. Add the remaining 1 cup sugar, the baking powder, and salt. Beat until combined, scraping bowl occasionally. Beat in eggs, milk, vanilla bean paste, and almond extract until combined. Beat in the ground almond mixture and as much of the flour as you can with the mixer. Stir in any remaining flour. Divide dough in half. Cover and chill at least 4 hours or until dough is easy to handle (dough will still be a little soft).
3. Preheat oven to 350°F. On a well-floured surface roll each portion of dough until ¼ inch thick. Using a 3- to 4-inch tree-shape or scalloped round cookie cutter, cut out dough. Place cutouts 1 inch apart on an ungreased cookie sheet. If desired, press very small rosemary sprigs onto cutouts.
4. Bake 8 to 10 minutes or just until edges are light brown. Remove; cool cookies on a wire rack. Brush a thin layer of Almond Glaze over cookies.

ALMOND GLAZE In a small bowl stir together 1 cup powdered sugar, 2 tablespoons milk, and ½ teaspoon almond extract. If necessary, stir in additional milk so glaze reaches a thin glazing consistency.

TO STORE Layer cookies between sheets of waxed paper in an airtight container; cover. Store at room temperature up to 3 days or freeze up to 3 months.

PER SERVING (1 cookie each) **CAL** 127, **FAT** 6 g (3 g sat. fat), **CHOL** 21 mg, **SODIUM** 73 mg, **CARB** 17 g (1 g fiber, 10 g sugars), **PRO** 2 g

Maple-Raisin Oatmeal Cookies

20g CARB

SERVES	30
HANDS ON	30 min.
TOTAL	45 min.

- ½ cup butter, softened
- ½ cup packed brown sugar
- ½ tsp. baking soda
- ¼ tsp. salt
- ⅓ cup pure maple syrup
- 1 egg
- 1½ tsp. vanilla
- ¾ cup all-purpose flour
- 1½ cups quick-cooking or regular rolled oats
- ¾ cup raisins or dried cranberries
- 1 cup powdered sugar
- 3 Tbsp. pure maple syrup

1. Preheat oven to 350°F. In a large bowl beat butter with a mixer on medium 30 seconds. Add brown sugar, baking soda, and salt. Beat on medium 2 minutes, scraping bowl as needed. Beat in ⅓ cup maple syrup, egg, and 1 tsp. of the vanilla. Beat in flour on low. Stir in oats and raisins.

2. Drop dough by teaspoons 2 inches apart onto an ungreased cookie sheet. Bake about 12 minutes or until edges are set and centers are still soft. Cool on cookie sheet 2 minutes. Remove; cool on wire rack.

3. In a small bowl stir together powdered sugar, the 3 Tbsp. maple syrup, and the remaining ½ tsp. vanilla. If necessary, add a milk or water, ½ tsp. at a time, to desired consistency. Drizzle over cooled cookies.

TIP If using regular oats, use an additional ¼ cup all-purpose flour.

TO STORE Place cookies in a single layer in an airtight container; cover. Store in the refrigerator up to 3 days.

PER SERVING *(1 cookie each)* **CAL** 112, **FAT** 4 g *(2 g sat. fat)*, **CHOL** 14 mg, **SODIUM** 69 mg, **CARB** 20 g *(1 g fiber, 13 g sugars)*, **PRO** 1 g

Pumpkin-
Almond
Macarons

temperature up to 3 days. Fill as directed.

PER SERVING (1 sandwich cookie each) **CAL** 65, **FAT** 2 g (0 g sat. fat), **CHOL** 0 mg, **SODIUM** 12 mg, **CARB** 11 g (1 g fiber, 10 g sugars), **PRO** 1 g

DOUBLE-ALMOND MACARONS
Prepare as directed, except omit pumpkin pie spice and fill cookies with Almond Butter Frosting instead of pumpkin butter. For Almond Butter Frosting, in a medium bowl beat 3 Tbsp. softened butter with a mixer on medium until smooth. Beat in 1 cup powdered sugar, 1 Tbsp. milk, and ½ tsp. almond extract until combined. Beat in 1 cup additional powdered sugar. If needed, beat in additional milk, 1 tsp. at a time, to reach spreading consistency.
PER SERVING (1 sandwich cookie each) **CAL** 97, **FAT** 4 g (1 g sat. fat), **CHOL** 3 mg, **SODIUM** 15 mg, **CARB** 16 g (1 g fiber, 15 g sugars), **PRO** 1 g

CHOCOLATE MACARONS
Prepare as directed, except substitute 2 Tbsp. unsweetened cocoa powder for pumpkin pie spice and fill cookies with chocolate-hazelnut spread instead of pumpkin butter.
PER SERVING (1 sandwich cookie each) **CAL** 72, **FAT** 23g (0 g sat. fat), **CHOL** 0 mg, **SODIUM** 7 mg, **CARB** 10 g (1 g fiber, 0 g sugars), **PRO** 2 g

Pumpkin-Almond Macarons

11g CARB

SERVES 30
HANDS ON 45 min.
TOTAL 1 hr. 35 min.

- 1¼ cups almond flour
- 1¼ cups powdered sugar
- 1 tsp. pumpkin pie spice
- 3 egg whites, room temperature
- ⅛ tsp. cream of tartar
- ¼ cup granulated sugar
- ¼ tsp. almond extract
- ½ cup pumpkin butter

1. Line two cookie sheets with parchment paper. In a food processor cover and process almond flour and powdered sugar 1 minute, stopping once to scrape mixture from bottom of bowl. Sift flour mixture, a little at a time, through a medium-mesh sieve into a bowl, pressing with the back of a spoon to pass through as much as possible. Discard any large pieces that remain in sieve (up to 1 Tbsp.). Stir pumpkin pie spice into flour mixture.
2. In a large bowl beat egg whites and cream of tartar with a mixer on medium 1 minute or until frothy. Gradually add granulated sugar, beating on high about 4 minutes or until stiff, shiny peaks form.

3. Gently fold flour mixture into egg whites until all of the flour mixture is incorporated (about 50 strokes), giving the bowl a quarter turn with each fold. Add almond extract. Continue folding and turning 2 to 3 minutes more, scraping down bowl, until batter is smooth and falls off spatula in a thin, flat ribbon. (Batter will be thin.)
4. Transfer batter to a large decorating bag fitted with a ¼-inch round tip. Pipe 1¼-inch circles 1 inch apart onto prepared cookie sheets. Lift and drop sheets five times flat against counter to release any air bubbles. Let stand 30 to 45 minutes or until tops of cookies are no longer sticky.
5. Preheat oven to 300°F. Bake about 18 minutes or until tops of cookies are set and shiny and rise ⅛ inch to form the ruffled edge called the "foot." Cool on cookie sheets on wire racks. Carefully peel cookies off parchment paper.
6. Spread pumpkin butter on bottoms of half of the cookies, using about ½ tsp. for each cookie. Top with remaining cookies, bottom sides down.

TO STORE Layer unfilled cookies between sheets of waxed paper in an airtight container. Store at room

Three-Ingredient Peanut Butter Cookies

9g CARB

SERVES 32
HANDS ON 20 min.
TOTAL 30 min.

- 1 cup sugar
- 1 cup peanut butter
- 1 egg

1. Preheat oven to 375°F. Grease cookie sheets or line with parchment paper. In a medium bowl stir together all ingredients until well mixed. Shape dough into 1¼-inch balls. Roll balls in additional sugar to coat. Arrange balls 2 inches apart on the prepared cookie sheets. Flatten by making crisscross marks with the tines of a fork.
2. Bake about 8 minutes or until edges are lightly browned. Cool 1 minute on cookie sheets. Remove; cool completely on wire rack.

PER SERVING (1 cookie each) **CAL** 78, **FAT** 4 g (1 g sat. fat), **CHOL** 6 mg, **SODIUM** 36 mg, **CARB** 9 g (0 g fiber, 8 g sugars), **PRO** 2 g

Three-Ingredient Peanut Butter Cookies

RECIPE GUIDE

Inside Our Recipes

Precise serving sizes (listed below the recipe title) help you to manage portions.

Test Kitchen tips are listed after the recipe directions.

When kitchen basics such as ice, salt, black pepper, and nonstick cooking spray are not listed in the ingredients list, they are italicized in the directions.

Ingredients
* Tub-style vegetable oil spread refers to 60% to 70% vegetable oil product.
* Lean ground beef refers to 95% or leaner ground beef.

Nutrition Information

Nutrition facts per serving are noted with each recipe.

Ingredients listed as optional are not included in the per-serving nutrition analysis.

When ingredient choices appear, we use the first one to calculate the nutrition analysis.

Key to Abbreviations
CAL = calories
sat. fat = saturated fat
CHOL = cholesterol
CARB = carbohydrate
PRO = protein

Handling Hot Chile Peppers
Chile peppers can irritate skin and eyes. Wear gloves when working with them. If your bare hands do touch the peppers, wash your hands with soap and warm water.

RECIPE INDEX

METRIC INFORMATION

The charts on this page provide a guide for converting measurements from the U.S. customary system, which is used throughout this book, to the metric system.

Product Differences

Most of the ingredients called for in the recipes in this book are available in most countries. However, some are known by different names. Here are some common American ingredients and their possible counterparts:

* All-purpose flour is enriched, bleached or unbleached white household flour. When self-rising flour is used in place of all-purpose flour in a recipe that calls for leavening, omit the leavening agent (baking soda or baking powder) and salt.
* Baking soda is bicarbonate of soda.
* Cornstarch is cornflour.
* Golden raisins are sultanas.
* Light-color corn syrup is golden syrup.
* Powdered sugar is icing sugar.
* Sugar (white) is granulated, fine granulated, or castor sugar.
* Vanilla or vanilla extract is vanilla essence.

Volume and Weight

The United States traditionally uses cup measures for liquid and solid ingredients. The chart below shows the approximate imperial and metric equivalents. If you are accustomed to weighing solid ingredients, the following approximate equivalents will be helpful.

* 1 cup butter, castor sugar, or rice = 8 ounces = 1/2 pound = 250 grams
* 1 cup flour = 4 ounces = 1/4 pound = 125 grams
* 1 cup icing sugar = 5 ounces = 150 grams

Canadian and U.S. volume for a cup measure is 8 fluid ounces (237 ml), but the standard metric equivalent is 250 ml.

1 British imperial cup is 10 fluid ounces.

In Australia, 1 tablespoon equals 20 ml, and there are 4 teaspoons in the Australian tablespoon.

Spoon measures are used for smaller amounts of ingredients. Although the size of the tablespoon varies slightly in different countries, for practical purposes and for recipes in this book, a straight substitution is all that's necessary. Measurements made using cups or spoons always should be level unless stated otherwise.

Common Weight Range Replacements

Imperial/U.S.	Metric
1/2 ounce	15 g
1 ounce	25 g or 30 g
4 ounces (1/4 pound)	115 g or 125 g
8 ounces (1/2 pound)	225 g or 250 g
16 ounces (1 pound)	450 g or 500 g
1 1/4 pounds	625 g
1 1/2 pounds	750 g
2 pounds or 2 1/4 pounds	1,000 g or 1 Kg

Oven Temperature Equivalents

Fahrenheit Setting	Celsius Setting*	Gas Setting
300°F	150°C	Gas Mark 2 (very low)
325°F	160°C	Gas Mark 3 (low)
350°F	180°C	Gas Mark 4 (moderate)
375°F	190°C	Gas Mark 5 (moderate)
400°F	200°C	Gas Mark 6 (hot)
425°F	220°C	Gas Mark 7 (hot)
450°F	230°C	Gas Mark 8 (very hot)
475°F	240°C	Gas Mark 9 (very hot)
500°F	260°C	Gas Mark 10 (extremely hot)
Broil	Broil	Grill

Electric and gas ovens may be calibrated using celsius. However, for an electric oven, increase celsius setting 10 to 20 degrees when cooking above 160°C. For convection or forced air ovens (gas or electric), lower the temperature setting 25°F/10°C when cooking at all heat levels.

Baking Pan Sizes

Imperial/U.S.	Metric
9×1 1/2-inch round cake pan	22- or 23×4-cm (1.5 L)
9×1 1/2-inch pie plate	22- or 23×4-cm (1 L)
8×8×2-inch square cake pan	20×5-cm (2 L)
9×9×2-inch square cake pan	22- or 23×4.5-cm (2.5 L)
11×7×1 1/2-inch baking pan	28×17×4-cm (2 L)
2-quart rectangular baking pan	30×19×4.5-cm (3 L)
13×9×2-inch baking pan	34×22×4.5-cm (3.5 L)
15×10×1-inch jelly roll pan	40×25×2-cm
9×5×3-inch loaf pan	23×13×8-cm (2 L)
2-quart casserole	2 L

U.S. / Standard Metric Equivalents

1/8 teaspoon = 0.5 ml	
1/4 teaspoon = 1 ml	
1/2 teaspoon = 2 ml	
1 teaspoon = 5 ml	
1 tablespoon = 15 ml	
2 tablespoons = 25 ml	
1/4 cup = 2 fluid ounces = 50 ml	
1/3 cup = 3 fluid ounces = 75 ml	
1/2 cup = 4 fluid ounces = 125 ml	
2/3 cup = 5 fluid ounces = 150 ml	
3/4 cup = 6 fluid ounces = 175 ml	
1 cup = 8 fluid ounces = 250 ml	
2 cups = 1 pint = 500 ml	
1 quart = 1 litre	